NATIONAL GALLERY OF ART

WASHINGTON, D. C.

NATIONAL GALLERY
OF ART
WASHINGTON, D. C.

JOHN WALKER

Director of the National Gallery of Art

HARRY N. ABRAMS, INC. · PUBLISHERS · NEW YORK

NOTE

Parts of this book have been previously published in *Art in America, Ladies' Home Journal, National Geographic Magazine, Twin Editions, Great Paintings of the World,* and certain National Gallery of Art publications and catalogues. I am very grateful for permission to reprint this material.

J. W.

CONTENTS

CHAPTER I

INTRODUCTION

Though the National Gallery of Art is the youngest of the world's great public galleries, in the character of its collections it resembles the oldest of the European museums. For, like the galleries of Paris, Vienna, Munich, Leningrad, and Madrid, it reflects the taste of discerning private collectors. They are the American successors to those princely amateurs who founded the national collections of Europe: the rulers of France, the Emperor Rudolph, the Archduke Leopold, Philip IV of Spain, Catherine the Great, and others. Thus, of roughly one thousand paintings and sculptures regularly exhibited on the main floor of the National Gallery of Art, more than eighty per cent have come from the Mellon, Widener, Kress, and Dale Collections. The Gallery also possesses over 22,000 prints and drawings, the larger part of which has been given by Mr Lessing J. Rosenwald. These are the principal benefactors. Many other gifts have also been received, but since the inauguration of the Gallery in 1941, it has bought only twenty-five paintings. All these purchases have been made from funds donated by public-spirited citizens. The treasures in the National Gallery, so speedily assembled, could in any case have been brought together in this century only through the generosity of private collectors. Great collections are formed most frequently by individuals, seldom by committees, and rarely by governments.

Some governments have at times even shown themselves more ready to disperse than to assemble works of art. Consider, for example, the history of Raphael's *St George and the Dragon,* one of the greatest treasures in the National Gallery of Art. In three

7

hundred years this panel has been twice sold by governments. It was first commissioned by Duke Guidobaldo da Montefeltro, the ruler of Urbino, as a present for Henry VII of England. The English King had made the Italian ruler a Knight of the Garter, and Raphael was told to paint on the armor encasing St George's leg the emblem of that knightly order. After the execution of Charles I, the revolutionary government of England sold this panel along with the rest of his collection. It was bought privately in France, where it remained until, under the shadow of the French Revolution, it was acquired by Catherine the Great and taken to Russia. Another revolution and another government, the U.S.S.R., again sold it, this time from the Hermitage, the museum of Leningrad, along with twenty other paintings, which Mr Mellon acquired for the National Gallery of Art. In the same way Hitler ordered to be sold from the German museums paintings which eventually entered the Kress and Mellon collections.

Many governments have had a fluctuating attitude toward their works of art. Sometimes they have looked upon paintings and sculpture as a form of national wealth, the equivalent of a gold reserve, intrinsically useful only to sustain the value of their currencies, but at other times paintings and sculpture have been promoted to the position of a cultural heritage. Today the pendulum has swung from improbable sales to impossible restrictions, and it is only with the greatest difficulty that important works of art, even though privately owned, can be exported from most European countries.

Therefore the National Gallery of Art, handicapped by having been established so recently, might have failed to attain its present eminence even if Congress had appropriated billions of dollars. To become a museum of the first rank it needed more than money. It needed the five great donations it received. Four of these were from people either born in Pennsylvania or residing there. It is an interesting fact that a majority of the outstanding collections of America have come from that state. Six of the greatest are the Mellon, Frick, Barnes, Rosenwald, Widener, and Kress collections. Andrew W. Mellon and Henry Clay Frick were Pittsburghers; Albert C. Barnes, Lessing J. Rosenwald, Peter A. B. Widener and Joseph E. Widener made Philadelphia their home; and Samuel H. Kress and Rush Kress were born near Allentown. Of these six collections four – the Mellon, Widener, Kress, and Rosenwald Collections – ended up in the National Gallery of Art. These four donations will be discussed later, but to understand their significance it is necessary to describe the slow growth of the idea and, finally, the realization of a national gallery in the capital of the United States.

CHAPTER II

GENESIS

Until recent times the American continent has been destitute of Old Masters. The leading artists of this country, from Copley in the eighteenth century to Mary Cassatt who died in 1926, have recorded their lamentations. There was nothing for them to study. They had to go abroad to learn to paint. The New World might afford political liberty, freedom of worship, and unsurpassed prosperity, but it did not offer models for their work. That grindstone of the achievements of the past against which they needed to polish their own attainments was nowhere to be found.

Not that Americans were indifferent to art. We seem always to have had a surprising passion for paintings. Like the Dutch in the seventeenth century we have eagerly commissioned portraits of ourselves, our possessions, our way of life and, in our mementos and memorials, our way of death. As John Neal, the first important American art critic, wrote in 1829, 'You can hardly open the door of a best-room any where, without surprizing or being surprized by, the picture of somebody, plastered to the wall and staring at you with both eyes and a bunch of flowers.'

But until the end of the last century Americans, with rare exceptions, had no time for connoisseurship—for that lust of the eye which, coupled with a sense of possession, leads to the formation of great collections. As John Adams, the second President of the United

States whose correspondence often contains prophetic truths, wrote to his wife in 1780: 'I must study politics and war, that my sons may have liberty to study mathematics and philosophy. My sons ought to study mathematics and philosophy, geography, natural history and naval architecture, navigation, commerce, and agriculture, in order to give their children a right to study painting, poetry, music, architecture, statuary, tapestry, and porcelain.' One can see the stages outlined by Adams clearly reflected in the changing conceptions, over a period of a century and a half, of the nature and role of a national gallery of art in this country.

The two or three generations that followed Adams were indeed interested primarily in science and the practical arts, though the crafts and portrait painting found widespread support. The Old Masters, however, continued to be out of reach. The nature of the collection of the Washington Museum, the first institution of its kind in the capital, is characteristic. The so-called museum, which was opened in 1836, consisted of two rooms in which the proprietor had arranged 'between 400 and 500 specimens.' These included objects of natural history, historical relics, coins, and miscellaneous art objects. Of the works of art exhibited, only three paintings, a portrait of Cardinal Mazarin, a *Massacre of the Innocents*, and a *Turkish Battle Piece*, all by unknown artists, are still traceable; but these indicate the type of minor painting collected in this country at the beginning of the last century.

In the following years the evolution foretold by John Adams gradually produced an increasing emphasis on the fine arts. The Washington Museum was incorporated into the National Institute, established in 1840. In the new museum, though natural history continued to be the major interest, the fine arts began to assume a greater importance. The Director of the Institute, the Honorable Joel R. Poinsett, was also Secretary of War, a bizarre combination of responsibilities, which suggests his transitional role in the chronology outlined by John Adams. In a speech delivered in 1841 the only American museum director ever to obtain cabinet rank (and the only museum director after whom a flower, the poinsettia, has been named) made an impassioned plea for the arts: 'Here, the people reign – all power is centered in them; and if we would have them not only maintain their ascendency, but use their power discreetly, no expense or pains should be spared to inspire them with a love of literature, and a taste for the fine arts. To effect this, the effort must be made here. It must originate at the seat of Government, and spread from this place over the populous plains and fertile valleys of the land.'

It was a noble and enlightened attitude. Poinsett, however, labored under a handicap. He had no way of spreading taste over 'the populous plains and fertile valleys.' Faced with the problem, he offered a brave though alarming solution. He recommended disseminating throughout the country copies of those 'pictures, statues, and medals,' which had been commissioned by Congress. Fortunately the project was never carried out. Nevertheless, throughout the nineteenth century the position of art in this country was improving. In the capital, improvement was aided by an unexpected bequest. An Englishman, James Smithson, left $550,000 to the United States for 'the increase and diffusion of knowledge among men.'

Every American has heard of 'The Smithsonian,' but few know who Smithson was. An Englishman of noble lineage, his father was the Duke of Northumberland. Fortunately for the United States the Duke philandered, and Smithson was born out of wedlock. Precluded by illegitimacy from assuming any of his father's titles, he was nevertheless brought up as a man of wealth and given the best possible education. He graduated from Oxford at twenty-one and a year later was made a member of the Royal Society of London, one of the youngest scientists upon whom this honor was ever conferred. His subsequent researches in mineralogy proved so significant that an ore, smithsonite, bears his name.

Except in the case of royalty a bar sinister has usually proved a bar; and Smithson found himself deprived of what he considered to be his rightful place in society. A deep bitterness poisoned his life.

'The best blood of England,' he wrote, 'flows in my veins; on my father's side I am a Northumberland, on my mother's I am related to Kings, but this avails me nought. My name shall live in the memory of men, when the titles of the Northumberlands and the Percys are extinct and forgotten.' This must have seemed a most unlikely hope. Yet, as an adjective at least his name has achieved immortality.

James Smithson died in Genoa in 1829. A nephew who had a life interest in the estate died six years later, and in 1835 President Jackson notified Congress of a legacy to the United States from an unknown Englishman who had never even visited this continent. No famous institution ever had an odder beginning than the Smithsonian Institution. One Congressman declared in a flood of oratory that it was below the dignity of the Republic to accept the bequest. In the words of Senator Preston of South Carolina, 'If an institution of this kind was desired, he [Preston] would prefer it to be established out of our own funds, and not have Congress pander to the paltry vanity of an individual. If they accepted this donation, every whippersnapper vagabond that had been traducing our country might think proper to have his name distinguished in the same way.'

John Quincy Adams, the sixth President of the United States, who had been elected to Congress after completing his presidential term, succeeded in persuading his fellow legislators that Smithson's far-seeing benefaction would prove a national asset; and in due course the legacy, entirely in gold sovereigns, was loaded on board a ship and landed in New York. Again difficulties arose over the testator's language. What did Smithson mean by that ambiguous statement that his bequest should be used 'for the diffusion of knowledge among men'? Did this imply an institute of advanced studies? Advocates were found for an agricultural school, a research laboratory, a meteorological bureau. But in the end it was decided that Smithson had in mind something of a more general nature. Finally in 1846, eleven years after the bequest was received, Congress established the Smithsonian Institution.

A board of Regents was selected and almost immediately adopted a resolution which provided that endowment funds should be appropriated for the 'procuring, arranging, and preserving of the various collections of the institution, as well of natural history and objects of foreign and curious research and of elegant art, as others.'

Art, it is evident, is still at the bottom of the hierarchy, below 'natural history and objects of foreign and curious research.' Though the Regents granted to art the adjective 'elegant,' they still did not grant to it much else. In half a century, apart from absorbing the National Institute in 1862, the only important support for art granted by the Smithsonian was $3,000 spent for the Marsh Collection of prints, an acquisition which today could be sold for many times its cost. Meanwhile, the other departments of the Smithsonian were growing with phenomenal rapidity.

A change, however, was about to occur. A portent was the publication by Franklin Webster Smith in 1891 (revised and enlarged in 1900) of *A Design and Prospectus for National Galleries of History and Art in Washington.* Though himself not an architect (he was a former hardware merchant), Franklin Webster Smith (1825–1911) had a hobby of making models of famous buildings and sights he had seen on his trips abroad; and one of his most famous reconstructions of ancient architecture, prior to the schemes for transforming Washington into a new Athens on the Potomac, was his Pompeia or House of Pansa in Saratoga Springs. Mr Smith's book is a mirror of the taste and culture of the United States at the turn of the century. Enthusiasm, grandiose conceptions, missionary zeal, mechanical inventiveness, and a typical desire for a short cut to all the benefits associated with the fine arts are reflected in his plans. It was proposed to erect within the District of Columbia a wonderful agglomeration of magnificent edifices, a whole city 'with walls and towers . . . girdled round.' These buildings were to be full-sized models of various monuments of all ages. They were to cover sixty-two acres southwest of the Washington Monument. They were to be constructed of Portland cement, and decorated with paintings corresponding to the styles of the various countries. Displayed within were to be copies of great works of art. The United States was to be represented on the principal site by a reconstruction of the Acropolis with a model of the Parthenon which, on the popular theory of the bigger the better, was to be one-half larger than the original. This 'pleasure dome' of art and culture was to have a device installed which might well, if adopted today, provide the solution to 'museum fatigue.' Mr Smith suggested that his National Galleries be provided with 'slow, automatic, moving seats facing both walls,' which he said, 'will be of great luxury, alike to casual observers and students.'

How incredible it seems that this vast, permanent World's Fair in the middle of Washington, our first concept of a national gallery, should have won widespread support! Yet members of Congress took it up, prominent architects helped with plans, and European museum authorities wrote letters of approval. In view of all this enthusiasm it is amazing that this fantastic national gallery was never built!

An assumption at the base of Smith's scheme, warmly approved by European museum directors, was that America must satisfy herself with copies. An eminent professor of architecture was quoted by Smith's supporters as saying that he 'should restrict a national institution to casts of antiquarian remains, considering the fictitious value of originals in comparison.' The argument was advanced that 'these reproductions were in every way as valuable for education as originals.'

Though reproductions represented a strong temptation – an easy access to treasures that otherwise seemed out of reach in this century – magnificent works of art began to be acquired in Europe and to cross the ocean. As few Americans intended to leave their collections to their descendants, a stream of these masterpieces gradually flowed to public galleries. But Washington, in spite of the establishment of the Corcoran Gallery of Art in 1869, a privately-endowed institution with many important paintings and sculptures, lagged behind half a dozen other cities.

In 1906 the courts decreed that the art department of the Smithsonian Institution should be the recipient of the Harriet Lane Johnston Collection, and was in fact the National Gallery of Art.

Other gifts and bequests were added to the newly christened department. Mr Charles Lang Freer, a railroad financier of Detroit and famous for his patronage of Whistler, went further and decided to build and give to the Federal Government a gallery for his own collection of Eastern art, and for the work of certain American painters he admired. Nevertheless, the Federal Government still lacked an adequate gallery of Western art; its National Gallery was still handicapped by its traditional position as an adjunct to a museum of natural history. The country had reached the third stage envisaged by John Adams, and the people were beginning to claim their right to study the fine arts, but the capital still could not provide the opportunities offered by such cities as Boston, New York, Philadelphia, Chicago, Cleveland, and Detroit.

The first real step toward the founding of an adequate national gallery was made by Andrew Mellon, as we shall see presently in dealing with his collection. It was during the period of his Secretaryship of the Treasury and afterward while Ambassador to the Court of St James's that he came to his important decision about the original National Gallery. He felt that it would always be handicapped by a position subordinate to the great scientific and historical collections of the Smithsonian Institution. He realized that the only solution was to establish a new gallery, in a building of its own, with its own endowment, its own appropriation from the Federal Government, and its own Board of Trustees. On the other hand, he thought it wise that the contemplated gallery should be placed under the aegis of the Smithsonian Institution, which had always been free from political interference. He offered to erect a building, to give his collection, and to provide an endowment on condition that Congress would appropriate funds to support the new museum. His offer was accepted and the necessary legislation was quickly enacted. Congress pledged the faith of the United States to the maintenance of the new Gallery; and a Board of Trustees, consisting of four ex-officio members, the Chief Justice, and the Secretaries of State and the Treasury, and the Secretary of the Smithsonian Institution—and five private citizens—constituted the governing authority.

CHAPTER III

THE BUILDING

In June 1937, ground was broken for the new Gallery. Mr Mellon died in August and during the next four years, between the Capitol and the Washington Monument, the Trustees of The A. W. Mellon Educational and Charitable Trust erected the largest marble building in the world. Mr Mellon had selected as architect John Russell Pope, and after his death in 1937, his associates Otto R. Eggers and Daniel Paul Higgins continued the work. It had been decided that the new edifice should be in the classical style predominant in Washington. The exterior was influenced by George Hadfield's Old District Court House erected in 1820. On the east and west ends are lofty portals and on the north and south monumental Ionic porticos. Otherwise the exterior is adorned only with niches and pilasters, and the beauty of the building lies in its marble masonry, delicately rose in color, and in its harmony of proportion.

Pope was an architect pre-eminent in his ability to handle classical forms dramatically. As the main feature of the Gallery he designed a rotunda with a great coffered dome upheld by towering columns of green-black marble. This central area, in its proportions, its concept of space, its classical orders, is a free adaptation of the interior of the Pantheon in Rome, though actually departing further from its model than, say, Bernini's church in Ariccia. Joined to the rotunda by halls for monumental sculpture are two garden courts where changing exhibitions of flowers, grown in the Gallery's greenhouses, are continuously displayed. Around these architectural features are grouped the rooms for paintings and smaller sculpture.

19

The building was intended to satisfy a desire on the part of the public often unrecognized. In this country there is a lack of the magnificent churches, public buildings, and palaces of Europe; and Americans living for the most part in apartments and small houses feel the need for buildings more sumptuous, more spacious, and less utilitarian than their everyday surroundings. The satisfaction of this desire has a psychological value as definite as it is difficult to analyze. From architecture that has dignity, splendor, permanence, people seem to gain an enhancement of their own personalities. There can be no doubt that, disregarding the collections, visitors receive great pleasure from the National Gallery simply as a beautiful building.

But there is always a danger that the museum building will dominate its contents. This, I believe, the National Gallery of Art has avoided. David E. Finley, the first Director, who greatly influenced all the plans, and I, who had just become Chief Curator when the building was begun, were determined that attention should be focused on the works of art. It seemed to us a mistake to clutter up the painting and sculpture galleries with antique furniture, statuary, tapestries, and other decorative arts, as is the practice in some museums. In the National Gallery the picture galleries are galleries of pictures; the sculpture galleries, galleries of sculpture. Commodious sofas there are; but these are to rest the weary, not to indicate the type of settle used by Lorenzo the Magnificent.

To avoid monotony and to harmonize with the styles of painting, we selected different backgrounds for the different rooms: plaster for the early Italian, Flemish, and German pictures; damask for later Italian paintings; oak panelings for Rubens, Van Dyck, Rembrandt, and the other Dutch; and painted paneling for the French, English, and American canvases. A suggestion of the architectural styles prevalent when these schools flourished is indicated in wainscoting, moldings, and overdoors.

But we kept in mind our basic goal: to permit the visitor a concentrated and undistracted scrutiny of each work of art. Therefore we decided to hang the pictures twice as far apart as one usually sees them in other galleries—a method of installation which has been generally commended though very little imitated. To achieve greater isolation for each painting in many rooms we used paneling. The separation thus afforded a second frame, so to speak, which we believe more than compensates for any loss of flexibility. How taste has changed in the arrangement of works of art in the last forty years, how the individual object has gained more and more isolation, is clearly illustrated in two photographs of the Widener Collection: as it was first shown at Lynnewood Hall, and as it now appears in the National Gallery of Art.

Thus the whole installation of the Gallery was determined by a basic assumption: that the work of art is not a specimen, not primarily a historical document, but a source of pleasure. Accepting this premise it seemed to us that the major purpose of the National Gallery of Art was to allow each painting, piece of sculpture, or other object of art to communicate to the spectator, with as little interference as possible, the enjoyment it was designed to give. An art gallery and a concert hall, we felt, have much in common: one affords delight to the eyes, the other to the ears.

The museum director and the conductor of an orchestra are also comparable: both present as satisfactorily as possible the works of others, both have an interpretative function to perform, much greater, of course, in the case of the conductor. But the museum director has a further responsibility which the conductor avoids. He must preserve what he presents. In recent years this task of preservation has been immeasurably aided by air conditioning. The National Gallery is the largest completely air-conditioned art museum in the world; and the system works so well that atmospheric variations can be controlled to within five degrees of relative humidity. This stability has proved a vital factor in increasing the longevity of paintings, especially those executed on wood. For all pictures are vulnerable to fluctuations of humidity. These changes cause the support–the substance on which the picture is painted–to expand and contract at a rate different from the expansion and contraction of the surface of the picture. Consequently, blisters and cracks occur, which in turn cause the pigment to flake and chip away. The National Gallery of Art has one of the largest collections in the world of early Italian paintings, which are especially fragile. Yet, because of the stability of the atmosphere, almost no restoration has been required once these pictures have grown accustomed to their environment.

CHAPTER IV

DONATIONS

A. *The Mellon Collection*

Andrew Mellon's father came from Ireland and settled in Pittsburgh, where he became a Judge of the Court of Common Pleas, and was active in real estate, coal, and banking. By the standards of the time he was a rich man. Thus, even in his youth Mr Andrew Mellon was able to buy an occasional picture; but, as he once noted somewhat wryly, his friends and business associates looked askance when he paid as much as a thousand dollars for one of his earliest purchases. Collecting in Pittsburgh in the 1870s was not encouraged. This hobby was looked upon as particularly strange in a young banker who was in other respects not only full of common sense but who was admired by the whole community for his financial acumen. Yet he and his close friend, Henry Clay Frick, who later established the Frick Collection in New York, persisted in their extravagance. They traveled to Europe together and continued to collect, buying works of art at the rate of a few thousand dollars a trip – expenditures which, as the years passed, increased by geometric progression until each had dispersed scores of millions of dollars on the most expensive of all pastimes.

Mr Mellon's collecting began with seventeenth-century Dutch and eighteenth-century English painting. Living a somewhat solitary life, he found his Dutch and English portraits companionable. With them he perhaps enjoyed imaginary friendships unspoiled by that sense of shyness he always felt with people. In the same way, his views of Holland and England opened windows on a world more attractive than the smoky atmosphere of Pittsburgh, where at night every aperture was covered with cheesecloth and all the furniture draped in sheets to keep out the constantly settling soot.

Mr Mellon looked a great deal at his works of art. He learned discrimination and developed a remarkably good eye. His standards, however, remained personal, even idiosyncratic. According to David Finley, who worked closely with him in forming his collection, 'he did not like dark pictures, especially those with black backgrounds; and he had an aversion to paintings depicting unpleasant and harrowing scenes.'

For many years Mr Mellon bought from only one dealer, M. Knoedler and Company; later he made a number of purchases from Duveen Brothers. But these two firms were the only ones with whom he dealt. It was a shrewd policy, for, as he was the principal patron of each dealer, he could count on being offered the best works of art each could procure. He never bought at auctions. In those days it was customary in America for the dealers to negotiate purchases. Few sales were made in any other way.

Mr Mellon's more concentrated collecting began after he had served some years as the Secretary of the Treasury in the Harding and Coolidge administrations. David Finley recalls that in 1927 Mr Mellon first told him that he had decided that Washington needed a national gallery and that he would provide its building, a nucleus of its collection, and an initial endowment. From that time on his purchases, though made with the utmost discretion, astounded the art market.

His greatest coup as a collector was his acquisition in 1930 and 1931 of twenty-one masterpieces from the Hermitage Gallery in Leningrad. These Soviet sales came about somewhat fortuitously. The whole story, so far as I know, has never been told. It begins with the sale of oil by the Soviet Union and the assistance given to it by the brilliant oil magnate, Mr Calouste Sarkis Gulbenkian. The Soviets were at that particular moment hard-pressed for sufficient foreign currency to pay off their short-term loans. They decided to raise the money by exporting oil, but in this very complicated operation they needed advice, and Mr Gulbenkian's proved indeed helpful. The affair was consummated so successfully that the Soviet officials asked what they could do in return. Mr Gulbenkian proposed that he be permitted to buy some of their works of art, which, he pointed out, would have the further advantage of increasing their reserves of hard currency.

The Commissars were delighted. Nothing could have suited them better than to have one of the richest men in the world turning their art into gold like some modern alchemist. But they realized that the sale of oil paintings was as unfamiliar to them as the sale of oil. They again decided to call in an outside adviser. They settled on Francis Matthiesen, a young but shrewd German art historian who had just begun a career as a dealer. In November 1929, in the greatest secrecy, they invited him to Russia, showed him every important work of art in Leningrad and Moscow, and finally asked him to make a list with values of the hundred greatest paintings in the Hermitage. They said they wanted to know which pictures from that collection should never be sold under any circumstances. Mr Matthiesen gave them his list and returned to Berlin.

A few months later he received an invitation to come to Paris to see Mr Gulbenkian. He had never heard of the gentleman but was told that he was a new and incredibly rich collector. The moment they met he was asked about his trip to Russia. Mindful of the secrecy of his mission, he denied that he had been there. Mr Gulbenkian berated him, and then showed him his collection, which very few people had seen. To Matthiesen's amazement he was confronted with a number of the masterpieces from the Hermitage which he had listed among the one hundred never to be sold. Realizing that his Russian sojourn had been disclosed, he admitted that these were the pictures he had listed as irreplaceable. After a long discussion he was asked by Mr Gulbenkian to act as his agent in further sales. Matthiesen refused. Years later Mr Gulbenkian told me of his chagrin at this refusal. Thus, for once, this most secretive of men had revealed a valuable secret. He foresaw that Mr Matthiesen would lead other collectors to this treasure-trove; and in his anger with himself for making one of the few mistakes of his life, he withdrew entirely from the Russian market, a decision he was always to regret.

Young Mr Matthiesen realized at once that he had stumbled on the Golden Apples of the Hesperides as far as art dealers were concerned. He soon ascertained that the Russians were willing to have him act on their behalf. But he felt he lacked experience and he knew he lacked capital for such a venture. In this crisis he turned to the partners of Colnaghi's, a leading London art dealer, and together they got in touch with the Knoedler partners.

Knoedler & Co. had an important contribution to make, an asset the others lacked. They had as client the world's leading art collector, Mr Mellon. He was approached with the proposal that in return for the necessary funds, they would offer him his choice of anything they bought, at cost plus a commission, modest in itself but, because of the magnitude of the deal, ultimately very profitable to them. Also, he was asked to advise them in their selection. He agreed and, in the end, purchased all the paintings they acquired. He paid what seemed a huge amount at the time but, what in the present market must be considered a reasonable price, since he was able to add to his collection some of the greatest masterpieces in existence. These included Raphael's *St George and the Dragon*, already mentioned, and the *Alba Madonna*, the Botticelli *Adoration of the Magi*, Perugino's *Crucifixion with Saints*, Titian's *Venus with a Mirror*, Veronese's *Finding of Moses*, the van Eyck *Annunciation*, the Velázquez *Study for Innocent X*, and numerous works by van Dyck, Frans Hals, and Rembrandt.

Shortly after these purchases from the Hermitage were made, Mr Mellon became American Ambassador to the Court of St James's, where he remained from 1932 to 1933. It was a happy year in his life. From the time of his earliest trips to Europe he had gone repeatedly to look at the pictures in the British National Gallery. It had become his favorite collection. The size, the installation, the high level of quality all appealed to him. He determined that it should be the model for the Washington National Gallery of Art. One might have seen this delicate, sensitive, impeccably-dressed figure, already in his late seventies, sometimes alone, sometimes accompanied by David Finley, intensely scrutinizing paintings, teaching himself to discriminate, trying always to learn what made certain works of art greater than others.

This world of aesthetic contemplation, however, did not last. The Depression arrived and Herbert Hoover went down in defeat. On the election of Franklin D. Roosevelt lawyers from the Department of Justice and the Treasury descended on Mr Mellon. Mr Roosevelt and his followers, who had victoriously overthrown twelve years of Republican supremacy, looked upon Andrew Mellon as a symbol of all they opposed. They were determined to discredit him. They asserted that he had committed fraud on his Federal income-tax return. On these grounds they attempted to procure a criminal indictment, but the grand jury flatly refused to indict. A civil trial to collect penalties then dragged on, overshadowing the last years of his life. When the court finally handed down the verdict, it was a complete vindication of any wrongdoing, but Mr Mellon was no longer alive.

Yet, during a trial of extraordinary bitterness, he never lost his stoical detachment, never permitted the cruelty of the attack to cause him to deviate from his purpose of building a great national gallery in Washington. In December 1936 he wrote President Roosevelt, 'My dear Mr President: Over a period of many years I have been acquiring important and rare paintings and sculpture with the idea that ultimately they would become the property of the people of the United States and be made available to them in a national art gallery to be maintained in the city of Washington for the purpose of encouraging and developing a study of the fine arts.' And on December 26, Mr Roosevelt replied, 'My dear Mr Mellon: When my uncle handed me your letter of December 22 I was not only completely taken by surprise but was delighted by your very wonderful offer ... This was especially so because for many years I have felt the need for a national gallery of art in the Capital ... Furthermore, your offer of an adequate building and an endowment fund means permanence in this changing world.'

All during the tax trial Mr Mellon continued to collect, spending vast sums to assemble the works of art he felt would provide the nucleus for the Gallery. In the last twelve months of his life he acquired twenty-six paintings, ranging from works by Cimabue and Masaccio to Gainsborough's *Landscape with a Bridge*. Only a few weeks before his death he acquired Duccio's *Nativity*, once part of the *Maestà* of the Cathedral of Siena. This marvelous panel had been exchanged by the Kaiser Friedrich Museum in Berlin for a German painting to satisfy the wishes of Hitler for more Teutonic art.

Mr Mellon wanted his collection to provide a framework on which the collection of the National Gallery of Art might grow. Therefore he intended his pictures to recapitulate the development of Western painting. His gift begins with a Byzantine Madonna of the thirteenth century and ends with a Turner landscape of the nineteenth century. Between these terminal paintings there is an example by almost every artist who strongly influenced the development of style. Though his collection contains only 115 pictures, exclusive of American portraits, these were chosen with such discrimination that they provide a nearly complete outline of seven centuries of European painting.

He did not continue his collecting into the second half of the nineteenth century. He rightly considered American collectors to be very rich in the work of the French Impressionists and Post-Impressionists, the most significant schools of the last hundred years, and he believed that the Gallery through gifts would ultimately receive an ample representation of these movements – a judgment which has been proved correct.

But American painting he did wish to provide and to that end he bought *en bloc* the most important private collection of American portraits ever assembled, the Thomas B. Clarke Collection. He knew that the quality of these portraits, ranging from our pioneer painters to Frank Duveneck, was uneven; but he wished the National Gallery of Art and a future National Portrait Gallery, which he hoped would be established, to be enriched by a judicious selection from among them.

Originally it was Mr Mellon's intention to restrict his gift to painting, but he came to the conclusion that to understand the development of Italian art it is also necessary to know the works of the great sculptors of the Renaissance. With this in mind, especially during the last months of his life, he began to acquire magnificent statues of the fifteenth and sixteenth centuries, when sculpture, in Florence, reached the peak of its development.

Like the collection of paintings, the number of pieces of sculpture he bought is small, just over a score, principally from the famous Dreyfus Collection. But in both painting and sculpture the quality of the works of art shows an exacting connoisseurship. Mr Mellon wished his collection to establish a measuring rod which would guide future Trustees in their acceptance of gifts for the Gallery. Thus he set himself the difficult task of acquiring nothing but masterpieces, an undertaking which can fail with even the greatest financial resources. Mr Mellon, however, succeeded.

Unfortunately he did not live to see his collection installed in the National Gallery. Thus he did not witness and enjoy that moment which would have meant so much to him, when, with all his paintings and sculptures in place, he might have said to himself in Louis MacNiece's words, 'Hundreds of windows are open . . . on a vital but changeless world, a daydream freed from doubt.'

B. *The Widener Collection*

Of the five principal donations to the National Gallery of Art, the Widener Collection is the only one which was assembled, for the most part, before 1920. Unlike the other gifts, it represents two generations of collecting. It was begun by Peter A. B. Widener and continued by his son, Joseph E. Widener. No American family has ever amassed greater treasures.

The Widener Collection might be said to have grown out of a close friendship and association between Peter A. B. Widener, William L. Elkins, his partner in numerous enterprises, and John G.

Johnson, their lawyer. Mr Johnson had become absorbed in collecting, and it was his passionate interest in paintings that, like a magnet, drew his two friends and clients into this costly hobby.

At first that elusive quarry, the masterpiece, escaped the elder Widener. His collection at one time consisted of 410 paintings; of these more than 300 were eventually discarded. But he and his son were indefatigable in their search for whatever they believed to be supreme. The story of the so-called Youssoupoff Rembrandts is characteristic. Peter A. B. Widener knew of the existence of the two portraits and was determined to get them. He traveled to Russia and managed in some mysterious fashion to make his way into the Youssoupoff castle, where he finally saw these two marvelous portraits painted by Rembrandt in old age. But the Prince, one of the richest men in Russia, who must have looked on an American millionaire as poor by comparison, refused to consider selling. Years passed, and the Russian Revolution took place. The son of the Prince Youssoupoff who had disdained Mr Widener's offer found himself an exile in London, deeply in debt. Peter A. B. Widener by then was dead, but Joseph Widener continued the quest for the Rembrandts. He made another effort to buy them, and eventually his terms were accepted, with the reservation that the Prince might repurchase the works of art if he found himself in a position to resume his former way of life. One day Prince Youssoupoff presented himself at the Widener estate with a check for 100,000 pounds and a request for the return of the portraits. Mr Widener was suspicious and refused. His suspicions were justified, for it was discovered later that Mr Gulbenkian had supplied the funds for the repurchase. Then followed a complicated lawsuit involving, as the principal piece of evidence, a cable from Prince Youssoupoff accepting Mr Widener's offer. Though the Widener lawyers knew the cable existed, after an exhaustive search they could not find it. Nevertheless, they persuaded the court of its existence, and Mr Widener won the verdict. Years later the cable was found among a sheaf of pedigrees of horses, Joseph Widener's major interest apart from art.

When Peter A. B. Widener died in 1915 he left his son the disposition but not the ownership of the collection. Under his will the Widener works of art could be given to a museum in Philadelphia, New York, or Washington, or they could be sold for the benefit of the Widener family. Meanwhile they were displayed at Lynnewood Hall where the Wideners lived, a house which over the years became a pilgrimage site to all who were interested in art.

Andrew Mellon and Joseph Widener in the 1930s discussed the proposed National Gallery and the future of the Widener Collection without a definite decision being reached. Several years later, after Mr Mellon's death, and when the construction of the Gallery was under way, David Finley went to Lynnewood Hall and urged Mr Widener to give his collection to the National Gallery in Washington. Mr Widener seemed inclined to do so. Then David Finley with his wonderful intuition of how to persuade donors to give collections, asked the architect Otto Eggers to make renderings of the rooms where the Widener Collection might be placed, showing each work of art installed. Joseph Widener was entranced, but he was still reluctant to decide. After an agonizing period of uncertainty, he finally offered to designate the National Gallery of Art the fortunate museum provided three conditions could be met: a) that the collection should be shown as a unit; b) that the entire collection including Chinese porcelain, Renaissance furniture, tapestries, ceramics, jewelry, and rock crystals, and French eighteenth-century decorative arts, books, and engravings be accepted; c) that the gift be without taxes of any kind to the Widener estate.

The Widener Collection was a museum in itself and its acquisition of greatest importance to the new National Gallery. The first condition, that the collection be shown as a unit would, however, have nullified Mr Mellon's desire for a strictly chronological installation. This principle of an arrangement showing the historical development of painting and sculpture has remained a basic Gallery policy; but it is one that has cost the National Gallery of Art two collections only a little less important than the Widener Collection. The first demand, therefore, the Trustees refused, and Mr Widener finally accepted a compromise which has been satisfactorily employed in

31

the case of other collectors. He agreed that the Widener Collection should not be shown in contiguous rooms; but in return the Trustees also agreed that when there were enough paintings by one artist or a single school of artists, these would be kept together. The location of the room in which they would be shown, however, would conform with the pattern of the Gallery's chronological arrangement. Thus all the Widener van Dycks are placed in one room, but this room is adjacent to another gallery containing further works by van Dyck from various collections. In a similar way the Widener English paintings are installed in two rooms, at the opposite end of the building, where there are other galleries devoted to this school.

The second condition, that all the important Widener works of art, including decorative arts be accepted, was easier to satisfy. The National Gallery is built on two floors. The main floor has a skylight with natural illumination in the daytime and artificial illumination at night. It provides ample space for a collection somewhat larger than the collection on exhibition in the National Gallery in London. The ground floor, beside areas for temporary exhibitions, a print cabinet, and storage rooms, offered an ideal location for the Widener decorative arts. Though such works of art fall outside the scope of the collection as planned by Mr Mellon, they represent some of the greatest masterpieces in the Gallery, objects of inestimable value—for instance, the Suger Chalice, one of the most renowned examples in the world of the minor arts of the Middle Ages, the Mazarin Tapestry, the outstanding illustration in the United States of the achievement of Flemish weaving about 1500, and a superbly chosen collection of Renaissance jewels, rock crystals, and Chinese porcelains.

The third condition, that the gift should be tax free, was the most difficult to fulfill. Pennsylvania was one of the states in the Union which assessed a tax on bequests made to charitable institutions located outside the state. Ironically, under the Pennsylvania law if Joseph Widener had decided to sell the Widener Collection for the benefit of his father's heirs, there would have been no tax of any kind; but if these works of art were to be given to the Federal Government, then a five per cent tax would have to be paid to Pennsylvania. Efforts were made by the Gallery to have this law altered, but to no avail. The Pennsylvania legislators proved obdurate and difficult. They refused to estimate the value of the collection until the Gallery had agreed to pay the tax, but to accede to this meant accepting an unlimited commitment. The problem therefore seemed insoluble.

President Roosevelt took a personal interest and sent a message to Congress asking that the tax to Pennsylvania be paid regardless of the amount. The bill was passed and may well represent the only blank check ever written by Congress. It was this blank check which finally made possible one of the greatest donations in the history of museums.

There is about the Widener Collection a certain unity of selection difficult to describe. Both father and son showed a concentration of rare intensity in their collecting. They were the type of devoted amateur that has become scarce in the world today. Though they sought advice from scholars and experts, the ultimate decision was always theirs, and for this reason, perhaps, they soon freed themselves from those fads and fashions that have characterized modern taste. Barbizon canvases, which once hid the walls of American houses under drifts of gray-green foliage, they avoided or disposed of, being satisfied with a few magnificent Corots. The present ubiquitous vogue of the Impressionists they anticipated by half a century. Manet's *The Dead Toreador* entered the collection in 1894, to be followed by important works by Degas and Renoir, at a time when these artists were still not fully appreciated even in their own country.

Yet the instinctive taste of the Wideners was for an earlier age and an earlier style. Their real feeling was for the grand manner: for the High Renaissance in Italy, for the seventeenth century in the Netherlands, and the eighteenth century in England. Their aesthetic sense was close to that of the English milords, those landed amateurs portrayed by Reynolds and Gainsborough, whose galleries showed their love of Raphael, Titian, Van Dyck, and Rembrandt. For it is the work of these masters of the grand style which both

Wideners tirelessly sought throughout Europe and which today makes up the great treasures of their collecting.

Like eighteenth-century connoisseurs, Mr Widener and his son felt no interest in the styles of the thirteenth and fourteenth centuries, so highly esteemed in our time. Castagno, Neroccio de' Landi, Lorenzo di Credi, Mantegna, along with a few other fifteenth-century artists, seemed sufficiently archaic to indicate the origins of the Italian school. One painting by each of these masters was acquired, but what paintings they are! The unparalleled shield by Castagno; the rare example of Sienese portraiture of the fifteenth century by Neroccio; the only existing self-portrait by Lorenzo di Credi; as well as one of the most marmoreal and exquisitely preserved of Mantegna's panels – these and a few superb paintings by less well-known artists represent the Quattrocento.

Similar panels one might occasionally have found hanging on the walls of great eighteenth-century houses; but wonderful as such paintings now seem, they would once have been considered, and perhaps should still be considered, secondary to other pictures in the Widener Collection, such as *The Small Cowper Madonna* by Raphael, which Lord Cowper bought in Italy nearly two centuries ago; *The Feast of the Gods,* that most harmonious, but enigmatic work of collaboration between Giovanni Bellini and Titian, which was formerly the greatest treasure in the collection of the Duke of Northumberland; and the *Venus and Adonis* by Titian, which so impressed John Evelyn, the seventeenth-century diarist, when he saw it hanging in Lord Sunderland's dining room three hundred years ago. No less pride would an eighteenth-century connoisseur have taken in the portraits by Van Dyck in the Widener Collection. Early in the nineteenth century Sir Robert Peel's agent in Genoa tried unsuccessfully to buy several of these, for they were always considered the finest paintings the brilliant young Flemish portraitist had left in Italy, but several generations were to pass before the Cattaneo and certain other Genoese families were willing to part with their heirlooms.

The climax of the Widener Collection, however, by eighteenth-century or contemporary standards, would unquestionably be found in the astounding array of canvases by Rembrandt. To this group belongs perhaps the supreme painting in the entire collection, Rembrandt's great landscape *The Mill*, once owned by Lord Lansdowne. Constable and Turner, whose works are also brilliantly represented in the collection, have left records of how much they owed to this example of nature seen in the grand manner.

One characteristic of eighteenth-century amateurs Mr Widener and his son escaped or outgrew: that tedious fondness for genre or still-life subjects by the lesser Dutch masters, those canvases which so often cover, from wainscot to ceiling, the walls of English country houses. Though Hals, Cuyp, Hobbema, Ruisdael, De Hooch, Potter, Steen, and both Ostades are included in the collection, they are represented by only a few major works. And to these names, so familiar in every eighteenth-century catalogue, must also be added Jan Vermeer of Delft, whose forty-odd surviving pictures were forgotten for two centuries. Two of the greatest treasures in the Widener Collection are by him—one a masterpiece of tranquillity and stillness, *A Women Weighing Gold*, and the other a masterpiece of technical brio, *Young Girl with a Flute*.

When the Widener works of art were being packed for shipment to the National Gallery of Art, I spent several days with Joseph Widener at Lynnewood Hall. He was old and partly paralyzed. His trained nurse would help him into the long gallery where the paintings were being removed, and as he watched this desolate scene of crates and packing materials his eyes would fill with tears. He wanted to see the treasures he and his father had brought together installed in their new setting, but at the same time their removal broke his heart. Fortunately he was strong enough to pay one last visit to the Gallery, and from a wheel chair he saw every work of art placed exactly as he wished. He died soon after this final visit to Washington.

The dismantling of the Widener house signified the end of an epoch. The brevity of the way of life represented by Lynnewood Hall has its own historical significance. Whereas the nobility of Europe enjoyed their collections for centuries, the Widener family is remarkable in the United States for having possessed their works of art for two generations. In the United States the undertaker and the museum director customarily arrive in quick succession.

C. *The Kress Collection*

Of the principal collections given to the National Gallery of Art, the Kress Collection has been brought together most recently. Though Samuel Kress began buying works of art as early as the 1920s, the great purchases were made between 1937, the year the Gallery was founded, and 1956. Moreover, it is the only collection formed to some extent under the influence of the staff of the Gallery – an influence minimal at first but one which steadily increased over the years.

A schoolteacher in his youth, Samuel Kress saved his salary until he was able to purchase a small stationery and novelty store in northern Pennsylvania. His enterprise succeeded, and he expanded, selecting the South and West for the chain of stores he later established. These proved to be immensely profitable; and partly for business reasons and partly for pleasure, he began to make annual trips to Europe.

He became a collector almost accidentally. He was not a man who could ever be idle; and that European ennui, which affects so many American businessmen vacationing abroad, impelled him to seek an outlet for his indefatigable energy. He was introduced to an Italian art dealer, Count Contini-Bonacossi; and through his contact with the Count, as Mr Kress affectionately called him, he was soon infected with the collector's virus, succumbing almost immediately to that passion from which he never recovered, much to the benefit of the United States and particularly of the National Gallery of Art.

But Mr Kress's collecting was, at the beginning, of a special kind. Perhaps because of his life as a storekeeper, he often referred to his works of art in a naïve but charming way as 'items.' These 'items' were to provide the most complete and systematic collection of Italian art ever brought together. He wanted to assemble works by all the unique geniuses of the Italian schools; but he also wanted their entourage, those lesser-known painters and sculptors whose work explains and gives scale to the greater artists. Thus the full development of Italian painting and sculpture would be revealed by the Kress Collection.

Such an emphasis on the morphology of art represents a shift in the focus of appreciation from Mr Mellon and Mr Widener. The Kress Collection, in its first phase, reflected a point of view which has grown out of the characteristic twentieth-century interest in art history. It showed the full effect of the scientific approach introduced into connoisseurship, especially of Italian art, by Morelli. This system of attributing paintings was perfected by Berenson, whose remarkable, intuitive scholarship made a deep impression on Samuel Kress. No collector has ever gone to greater efforts to discover correct attributions than Mr Kress. In the dossier of nearly every object which he gave the Gallery are written opinions by Berenson, Fiocco, Longhi, Van Marle, Perkins, Suida, and Adolfo Venturi.

Samuel Kress's first purchases of Italian art were made in the most logical place, in Italy, and principally from his mentor in collecting, Count Contini-Bonacossi. But he discovered that the Italian private collections had long before yielded their greatest treasures either to the museums of their own country or to the collections of England, France, and Germany. He realized that if he were to bring together distinguished works not only by minor artists but also by the great masters, he would have to search beyond the wares being offered by a single Italian dealer. This realization, however, presented him with a dilemma. When he began collecting, he once told me, Mr Mellon dominated the international art market, and everything was offered to him first. Mr Kress was reluctant to buy what had already been, he suspected, turned down. He therefore refused to trade for many years with the principal dealers. With the death of Andrew Mellon in 1937 the situation changed, and Samuel Kress became the most important private collector in the world.

Each rise of the tide of economic prosperity in the various countries has left behind incrustations of beauty; and very little of the residuum of this treasure can be removed. In recent years, through increased export restrictions, these possessions have become still more firmly embedded. It is remarkable that Samuel Kress, forming his collection so late in history, could have found so many masterpieces still susceptible to the ebb and flow of wealth. But private collections in England yielded the noble Allendale Giorgione and the uncompromising *Portrait of a Condottiere* by Giovanni Bellini; in France a number of eighteenth-century paintings included the rare Boucher portrait of Madame Bergeret; and in Germany, in this case from museums, the Filippo Lippi *Madonna and Child* and the Raphael *Portrait of Bindo Altoviti.*

In Europe it is customary to think that works of art cross the Atlantic in only one direction. During the Depression, however, a number of the United States' greatest artistic possessions returned to Europe. For economic laws, which govern the movement of works of art, have not always been in our favor. In the thirties when our gold reserves were being drawn to Europe, their magnetic force pulled from us, among other masterpieces, the Mackay Sassettas (now in the National Gallery, London), the Kahn Carpaccio and Frans Hals and the Morgan Ghirlandaio (now in the Thyssen Collection, Lugano), all supreme achievements by these artists.

Only the purchases made by a few American private collectors, among whom Andrew Mellon and Samuel Kress were outstanding, checked this outflow of works of art from the United States. Mr Kress stopped further exportation of the Mackay and Kahn pictures, he bought most of the Goldman Collection, and many fine paintings from the collections of Robert Lehman and Dan Fellows Platt. Thus the original Kress Collection contained large parts of five of the most important private collections of Italian art formed in this country.

Though Samuel Kress took over Andrew Mellon's position as the United States' greatest collector, he had no intention of giving his collection to the museum Mr Mellon had established. The fact that in the end the Kress Collection came to Washington was almost a matter of chance. In the winter of 1938 while the Gallery was being erected, two friends, Herbert Friedmann, the Curator of Birds at the Smithsonian Institution, and Jeremiah O'Connor, the Curator of Painting at the Corcoran Gallery, made a trip to New York, intent on their favorite pastime, seeing as many private collections as possible. On this expedition they arranged to visit the Kress Collection, at that time scarcely known. Though neither was an expert in Italian art, they were astute enough to realize what Samuel Kress had already collected. On their return they described the extraordinary paintings and sculpture they had seen to David Finley. They went further and wrote Mr Kress, urging him to give his collection to Washington. They knew he was contemplating a private museum like the Frick Collection, and they argued eloquently against such a donation and in favor of a museum supported by the Federal Government where, they pointed out, the Kress Collection would be seen by more persons and have a more secure future. The result of the correspondence was an invitation from Samuel Kress to David Finley, asking him to come to New York to discuss the new museum in Washington.

Mr Kress and Mr Finley had met once on shipboard, though with characteristic modesty Samuel Kress had scarcely mentioned his collection. When the new Director of the National Gallery of Art saw what his steamship companion had brought together, he realized the collection must be procured for Washington. He had arrived at three in the afternoon; he left at ten in the evening. During those seven hours, with his inimitable powers of persuasion, he induced Samuel Kress to give up his plan for a private museum for which property was already under option and architectural drawings prepared, and to donate everything of significance in his collection to the National Gallery of Art. Had David Finley arrived only a few weeks later the Kress Collection would have remained on Fifth Avenue in its own building.

Instead, before the opening of the Gallery, in 1941, more than 450 paintings and sculpture were selected for Washington, partly for a permanent collection and partly for a study collection. It must have been very hard for Samuel Kress to face parting with all these works of art, for in many ways his paintings and sculpture were for him a substitute for the children he never had. After the final selection for Washington had been made, David Finley said to me, as we were leaving the Kress apartment, that our new friend seemed to look upon us with the questioning and dubious reflection of a father estimating the character of his future sons-in-law. It was an astute observation, and this somewhat delicate relationship continued for several years. About once a month we would go to New York, and Mr Kress would walk with us on the terrace of his penthouse or sit with us in his living room, where the blank walls seemed to accuse us of the treasures which had been removed. We would discuss the collection: how it looked, how it could be improved. Even in the last tragic years, when he was almost completely paralyzed, any mention of the National Gallery of Art would stimulate him to the effort of a reply. In the end we knew to our great joy that he was satisfied with the disposition of his collection, which he had originally looked on with considerable doubt.

After Samuel Kress was stricken, his much younger brother, Rush Kress took over the direction of the Samuel Kress Foundation and devoted much of its resources to collecting for the National Gallery of Art. For a decade after the war the art market received a new and unexpected influx of important works. During these years it was a 'buyer's market.' It is difficult to believe that comparable opportunities will arise again.

Rush Kress began his great purchases with a constantly repeated statement that he had no real interest in collecting but was simply completing a plan begun by his brother. Urged on by the Director of the Foundation's artistic program, Guy Emerson, and by Mario Modestini, the Curator of the Kress Collection, he grew fascinated by the quest for masterpieces. Often in carrying out the enrichment of his brother's collection, his judgment proved better than that of his advisers; but advice he did take, and almost for the first time the staff of the National Gallery of Art was consulted. Between 1945 and 1956 the Kress Foundation spent more than twenty-five million dollars on works of art. As the Gallery had the first choice of nearly all acquisitions, and considerable influence on their selection, this vast sum of money was in many ways a purchase fund, undoubtedly the largest capital expenditure dispersed in so short a time in the history of museums.

During the war a number of paintings were sent to the United States for safekeeping, and from among these Rush Kress was able to make exceptional purchases. From the Cook Collection he acquired seventeen pictures, including the famous *Adoration of the Magi* by Fra Angelico and Fra Filippo Lippi; from the Thyssen Collection the wonderfully preserved *St Veronica* by Memling, and other paintings; and from the collection of Count Cini, the Botticelli portrait of *Giuliano de' Medici* and the Gozzoli *Dance of Salome.*

After the war, at Rush Kress's instigation dealers went to Europe in a continuing search for paintings and sculpture. This resulted above all in magnificent acquisitions from the greatest of Viennese collections, those of Count Czernin and of Prince Liechtenstein. Moreover, whatever of outstanding importance came on the New York, London, or Paris markets was likely to be offered first to the Kress Foundation. The purchases in these years altered the character of the Kress Collection. More masterpieces were acquired and less attention paid to the minor Italian artists. The schools north of the Alps received new emphasis. A room devoted to German masters was assembled; two rooms of early Flemish and Hispano-Flemish paintings were added. Two galleries of seventeenth- and eighteenth-century French paintings supplemented those Samuel Kress had given; and Spanish, Dutch, and later Flemish pictures were bought.

Some idea of the magnitude of the purchases made between 1945 and 1956 by the Kress Foundation under Rush Kress's leadership may be gained from the Kress exhibitions held in 1951 and 1956 to celebrate the tenth and fifteenth anniversaries of the opening of the National Gallery of Art. In the two exhibitions there were 208 paintings and 46 pieces of sculpture. From these two shows the Kress Foundation offered the National Gallery of Art the choice of as many works of art as would strengthen and enrich the collection in Washington. The Gallery finally decided to retain 167 paintings and all the sculptures.

The rapid expansion of the Kress Collection presented the Gallery with an unsual problem. There was a danger that the collection in Washington might grow too rapidly, with undue duplication, with too many minor masters, and with unwarranted emphasis on the Italian schools. Rush Kress was well aware of the law of diminishing returns, which plagues museums with collections insufficiently distilled. He decided that his brother's conception of a study collection and a permanent collection, both located in Washington, was not the most efficient way to utilize the vast number of paintings and sculpture the Kress Foundation had acquired. He concluded that works of art in storage are of little use; whereas the same paintings and sculpture shown in a community deficient in art might have a profound effect. He therefore determined to make important donations to eighteen museums in cities stretching from Miami in the East to Honolulu in the West. He bought a number of important works for these galleries, and asked that the National Gallery of Art return to the Foundation in exchange for new gifts whatever it could spare from the Kress Foundation's previous donations.

The staff of the National Gallery of Art was thus presented with one of the most fascinating series of decisions in museum history. To discuss only paintings, the Kress Foundation owned over thirteen hundred canvases and panels, of which there were at least six hundred up to the standard of the National Gallery of Art. The space decided upon for the Kress Collection in Washington, more than a third of the main floor of the Gallery, would hold without crowding between 350 and 400 pictures. To reduce the Kress Collection to the present 377 paintings required eliminations which were often heartbreaking. But these were made less distressing by the realization that the 250 or more pictures surrendered by the Gallery would be enjoyed elsewhere in the United States.

Though the Kress Collection has been dispersed in this way, it will shortly be recorded in a seven-volume catalogue. These books will reunite and present to the world one of the greatest collections formed in this century. That the most significant part of this collection should have ended in Washington has helped to give the National Gallery of Art its high rank among museums.

D. *The Rosenwald Collection*

The fourth Pennsylvania collection to come to the National Gallery of Art was given by Lessing J. Rosenwald, a retired businessman who was for a time Chairman of the Board of Directors of Sears, Roebuck & Co. As the Rosenwald Collection consists almost entirely of prints and drawings it falls outside the scope of this book, although one watercolor by William Blake is reproduced to afford a token representation.

From the beginning Lessing Rosenwald has sought excellence rather than volume. Nevertheless he has brought together over seventeen thousand woodcuts, engravings, etchings, mezzotints, lithographs, and prints in other media. This is not an enormous collection, but considering that it was assembled by one collector and that the impressions are as fine as those to be found anywhere, it is an amazing achievement. In thirty years a single individual has formed a collection rivaling in quality if not in quantity the most important print cabinets of Europe.

In the past some print collectors, like the Abbé de Marolles wanted every print ever executed. In the seventeenth century, when he lived, one hundred thousand impressions would have represented print making completely. Today millions of examples would be required and such comprehensive collecting would be folly. Selectivity has become essential. Mr Rosenwald has discriminated carefully, basing his judgment on four criteria: beauty, content, rarity, and above all quality. As he has said himself, 'Quality is infinitely more difficult to attain than quantity. It is dependent on at least two variables, the ability to recognize the excellence of an impression from experience and knowledge and the availability of fine prints.'

Print collecting requires a special erudition. A discriminating eye, though basic, is in itself insufficient. There are matters of rarity, brilliance of impression, paper, margins, states, innumerable facts which the collector must know. In all these matters Mr Rosenwald's knowledge is exceptional.

In recent years the availability of outstanding prints and drawings has been on the whole greater than that of paintings or sculpture. There have been wonderful opportunities of acquisition from European collections like that of Count Harrach of Vienna, and from many of the European print cabinets which, since the war, have been increasingly inclined to dispose of their duplicates. Moreover, as prints and drawings are easy to transport, refugees from Nazi and Communist persecution have brought these precious leaves of paper to the auction rooms of Europe and America. Consequently, in some areas of print collecting Mr Rosenwald has assembled examples unmatched elsewhere. His collection of fifteenth-century wood and metal cuts, for example, is one of the finest of its kind in the world. An entire year's collecting is rewarded if a dozen excellent impressions of these rare prints can be found. Yet, because of a few extraordinary opportunities he has assembled over seven hundred examples, many of which are unique. There are other areas of print collecting in which the Rosenwald Collection is outstanding: engravings by the Master E. S., Schongauer, Dürer, Lucas van Leyden, and Nanteuil, to select a few artists.

Lessing Rosenwald has built a small museum near Philadelphia where the collection is housed at present. The Gallery itself has its own print rooms, to which prints and drawings are brought from this main depository as exhibition or study requires. Also traveling exhibitions, circulated throughout the United States, are arranged from the Rosenwald Collection. Last year thirty-five exhibitions of Rosenwald prints toured the country.

The Rosenwald Collection has been constantly augmented, and, since it was presented to the National Gallery of Art in 1943, it has more than doubled in size. This great donation deserves a more detailed treatment than is possible in the present book, which deals only with the paintings in the National Gallery of Art, but a full discussion will have to await a publication concerned specifically with prints and drawings.

E. *The Chester Dale Collection*

The sources of the principal donations to the National Gallery of Art are interestingly varied. Andrew Mellon bought from only two firms, M. Knoedler and Company, and Duveen Brothers. The Wideners and the Kresses were patrons of all the important art dealers in Europe and America. But Chester Dale alone was shrewd enough to augment his collection by becoming the partner of a dealer–the Galerie Georges Petit, one of the best-known companies dealing in Impressionist and Post-Impressionist canvases. This allowed him to scrutinize what was going on behind the scenes. His knowledge of the world centers of the art trade–57th Street in New York, Bond Street in London, and the rue la Boëtie in Paris–was unique among American collectors. It enabled him to enter the art market with complete assurance and to carry off, from dealers, private collectors, and the great auctions of Europe and America, treasures unsurpassed in their field.

Chester Dale, who died while this volume was in preparation, began life, however, collecting not great works of art but inactive and unlisted railroad mortgages. From that he progressed, as senior partner of W. C. Langley and Co., to collecting the controlling interest in certain public utility companies. Gifted with an amazing memory, and a quick, intuitive judgment, he pioneered with success in a field of investing then relatively unfamiliar, even to the investment bankers of his generation. Red-headed, wiry, sparkling with energy, and vital, Chester Dale must have been a formidable opponent among the financiers of his time. Wall Street was a challenge to him, a place to play a game with skill and daring. He played well, and ultimately retired to devote his intensely competitive nature to a different game, to the connoisseurship of works of art.

Here he was fortunate enough to receive indispensable assistance. Maud Dale, his first wife, was a painter and art critic who would have had a successful career in either field, had her days not been fully occupied arranging art exhibitions and finding paintings for her husband to buy. In the early years of their collecting it was she who would point to the quarry; Chester Dale would track it down and secure it. Masterpieces have their own protective coloration and are not always easy to discern. But Chester Dale's perceptive instinct soon developed, and with its development came a passion for works of art equaled by few collectors. His paintings, and the National Gallery of Art, became the major interests of his life. He gave unstinted devotion to both. For it was the essence of his character to commit himself entirely.

When Maud Dale died in 1953 one might have supposed that he would stop collecting. They had worked so closely together that the collection was in a way a joint enterprise. But such a supposition would have been wrong. He continued buying. In spite of the growing scarcity of masterpieces, some of his greatest acquisitions were made after her death.

The great period of purchase by Mr and Mrs Dale, however, took place during the 1920s. This was a time when the values of stocks and bonds were increasing daily until they were inflated beyond all reason; whereas the prices being paid for the work of the Impressionist and Post-Impressionist painters, whom the Dales especially collected were, though costly, excellent investments in relation to the market today. When the crash came, securities fell to a fraction of their former prices; but the value of French painting held up remarkably well, supported greatly by Chester Dale's continuing purchases. Since 1929 stocks have risen to an average somewhat less than twice their previous high; whereas French paintings now bring many times the highest prices ever paid in the twenties. Of all the collections in the Gallery, judged in purely monetary terms, the Chester Dale Collection has had far and away the greatest increase in value.

In the formation of his collection, Mr Dale from the beginning had a single aim in view: to show the brilliance of French painting during the last 150 years.*

In the illustrations which follow the reader can see in a wonderful panorama the development of two centuries of French painting, beginning with Rococo artists such as Boucher and Drouais, becoming more serious with Chardin, and even doctrinaire with David. Then follows the Romantic movement represented by Delacroix, a movement which led to a deeper appreciation of nature. Corot was the outstanding exponent of this new feeling for natural beauty. Among French landscape painters of the nineteenth century he is supreme, and the Chester Dale Collection represents his work at its best.

His *View Near Volterra* leads the eye into the scene by subtle transitions of detail and color, until one feels the exhilarating sweep of space, the great wash of air that lies between the shaded foreground and sunlit horizon. This same alertness of vision appears in the *Forest of Fontainebleau*–a picture Corot unsuccessfully tried to repurchase to present to the Louvre. *Agostina,* on the other hand, illustrates his mastery of figure painting, his ability to select precisely the significant lighted and shaded planes which suggest the solid form of this monumental woman, who like the women in the frescoes of Piero della Francesca, seems representative of an archetypal femininity. This triad of masterpieces by Corot marks one of the peaks of Mr and Mrs Dale's collecting.

The magnificent assemblage of works by Impressionist artists marks another peak. Among these is Manet's *Old Musician,* the most ambitious undertaking in size, number of figures, and complexity of design he ever attempted. Another landmark is Degas' *Four Dancers,* executed about 1899 when, with failing eyesight but with ever-increasing genius, the greatest draftsman of the Impressionist group was beginning to turn from oil to pastel, a technique which

---

*Chester Dale also collected and gave to the Gallery a number of works of earlier painters who influenced the masters of the last century: El Greco, Tintoretto, Rubens, Zurbaran, Boucher, and others, as well as a remarkable group of American paintings.

seems to have influenced this, one of his last and most distinguished canvases. Among the most popular paintings in the Gallery, judged by the sale of reproductions, is also an Impressionist work from the Dale Collection, Renoir's *Little Girl with a Watering Can*. The Dale Collection also contains works by practically all the other masters of Impressionism, including a large number of canvases by Monet, and important groups of pictures by Mary Cassatt, Berthe Morisot, Sisley, and Pissarro. Post-Impressionist canvases begin with Cézanne, Van Gogh, Gauguin, and the *douanier* Rousseau. Outstanding among these are Cézanne's *Still Life*, one of the greatest rhythmic designs the artist ever conceived, and Van Gogh's *La Mousmé*, a beautiful study of a young Provençal girl. Even taking into consideration the richness of America in Impressionist and Post-Impressionist paintings, the Chester Dale Collection remains one of the greatest collections of nineteenth- and twentieth-century French paintings ever assembled anywhere in the world.

F. *Other Individual Donations*

It is difficult for Europeans to realize that, with one or two exceptions, all American private collections with any considerable number of important Old Masters dating before 1800, have now been given to museums. The National Gallery of Art will never, in all probability, receive another Mellon, Widener, Kress, Dale, or Rosenwald donation, for under present circumstances it would be impossible to form such collections. In the future the growth of the Gallery will depend upon individuals who will give smaller groups of paintings or even single pictures. Already over a hundred collectors have made such gifts. Most of these donations have been either of American paintings or of French painting of the last century, two areas in which private collections in this country still possess fantastic riches. These gifts have varied in number from the unique collection of 215 American primitives given by Colonel and Mrs Edgar W. Garbisch, to a single great canvas by Manet, the *Gare St-Lazare*, bequeathed by Mr Horace Havemeyer.

There have also been distinguished gifts of Old Masters such as the Bellini, Boltraffio, Tintoretto, Cranachs, and Strigels, donated by Mrs Ralph Harmon Booth of Detroit; the superb portraits by Goya and other paintings given by Mrs Peter B. Frelinghuysen, who is the daughter of one of the greatest of American collectors, Mrs Henry O. Havemeyer; and the magnificent English paintings donated by the family of Governor Alvan T. Fuller of Massachusetts, to mention only a few.

Certain donations have been motivated in interesting ways. An economist and former member of the Federal Reserve Board, Mr Adolph Caspar Miller, used to come to the Gallery regularly and sit on a sofa facing the self-portrait of Rembrandt (reproduced on p. 185). A few weeks before he died I saw him in his usual place. He said he wanted to speak to me, and told me of his decision to leave his collection and a large donation to the National Gallery of Art. He explained that he had only one motive in making the bequest, namely to repay what he had learned from years of scrutiny of a single portrait. It was a bequest really to Rembrandt, and Mr Miller could think of no other way of expressing his gratitude.

Some of the bequests to the Gallery have been unusual. Mrs Lillian S. Timken of New York, for example, left her large collection to the National Gallery and the Metropolitan Museum in New York, without indicating which works of art should go to which institution. The Directors tried to divide the collection into equal groups, but in the end the Presidents of the two Boards of Trustees had to toss a coin for works by such artists as Moroni, Titian, Rembrandt, Van Dyck, Rubens, Boucher, Fragonard, Turner, and others.

Another unusual legacy was received from Mr Edward E. Mac-Crone of Detroit. He left in trust for the Gallery a considerable sum of money to be invested in bonds and common stocks until the year 2059, when the accrued capital will be turned over to the National Gallery of Art. Assuming the world to be still intact and conditions not too greatly changed, the Gallery a hundred years hence will derive from this bequest perhaps the largest purchase fund ever known.

There have also been friends who have come to the financial

assistance of the Director when a notable work of art has been offered for sale. Through her very generous donations, Miss Syma Busiel of Chicago has made it possible to acquire outstanding works of art for the Gallery. The W. L. and May T. Mellon Foundation and Mrs Maude Monell Vetlesen, of New York, have bought important American paintings at the Gallery's request; and Mrs Ailsa Mellon Bruce, the daughter of the founder of the Gallery, has shown outstanding generosity on many occasions and in many ways. Thus the Gallery even in the present 'seller's market' has always been in a position to compete for whatever painting or sculpture of exceptional merit has been offered for sale.

Purchases and gifts, apart from those of the principal benefactors of the Gallery, occupy less than twenty per cent of the present exhibition space. Another quarter of the Gallery remains for future expansion, and as individual collectors continue to make contributions, this area will be completed. When fully occupied, the main floor of the Gallery will exhibit approximately twelve hundred paintings, hung in accordance with the unusually large amount of space per picture which we believe to be desirable. This would seem to be the maximum number of paintings which will not unduly fatigue and bewilder the visitor. To have been given three-quarters of this number, in less than twenty-five years, and to have maintained a standard of quality as high as that of any museum in the world, is a measure of the generosity of American private collectors.

CHAPTER V

ACTIVITIES

A. *Education*

The visual arts have begun to play an increasingly important role in American education. Primary schools, secondary schools, colleges, and graduate schools all over the country are teaching painting and sculpture, and to a lesser extent the history of art.

This has created responsibilities and opportunities for museums. In no area is creativity more easily shared than in art. A work of art exists for us today as a self-contained entity whose original purpose was communication, communication not invalidated by the obsolescence of theory, as in science; or by the barrier of language, as in literature; or, even, by the mediation of a performer, as in the sister art of music. At the National Gallery of Art one looks at an image put on canvas by Rembrandt's own hand, and one contemplates greatness directly.

It is the purpose of the Gallery's Educational Department to make people aware of the vast reservoir of pleasure and enlightenment the collections represent. We have established in the Gallery Educational Department two educational divisions, one to look after visitors to the Gallery, the other for extension activities. The total staff devoted to educational work numbers twelve. Each day there are three types of tours: general tours of the whole collection, special tours dealing with a special field or a single school, and a lecture on a particular painting or sculpture. These are free and are attended annually by over forty thousand people. The Educational Department also trains volunteer docents from the Junior League and the American Association of University Women. These in turn work closely with the schools near Washington and take about 60,000 school children a year through the Gallery.

Many persons, however, prefer to wander through the collections by themselves. To allow them to listen to talks about the works of art at their own volition, transistor radios are available. These pick up continuous broadcasts on paintings and sculpture in thirty-one galleries. Last year 1,300,000 persons came to the Gallery and nearly 90,000 used this electronic guide system.

For those who would rather read than listen there are, in many rooms, leaflets describing the works of art in that particular gallery. They are free and can be taken home. Over 2,000,000 of the leaflets are distributed annually; and it is interesting to note that though we expected considerable litter from these myriad sheets of paper, almost none are thrown away. Our visitors seem to realize that, when assembled from all the galleries, they form a free handbook of the collection and are therefore worth preserving.

On Sunday afternoons there are free lectures in the auditorium given by authorities on different aspects of art. A series of six lectures, known as the A. W. Mellon Lectures in the Fine Arts, is delivered annually. These lectures are subsequently published by the Bollingen Foundation, established by Paul Mellon, the son of the founder of the Gallery.

As the Gallery is supported by taxpayers throughout the country we feel a special obligation to emphasize our extension services. We circulate to every state in the Union traveling exhibits, Gallery films, and slide lecture sets, all with written or recorded texts. These are lent free of charge except for transportation costs. Last year the Extension Service of the Gallery reached approximately a quarter of a million people. We hope soon, through a new plan involving the school systems of the various states, to increase our audience to many times that figure.

An interesting educational instrument located at the Gallery is the Index of American Design. During the Depression in the mid 1930s the Government, wishing to help artists, organized over 660 painters throughout the United States and gave them the task of recording the decorative arts and crafts of this country from the seventeenth century to the end of the nineteenth century. A remarkably exacting technique of watercolor rendering, formerly evolved to illustrate Egyptologists' finds, was taught to these artists. The resulting facsimiles of textiles, furniture, ceramics, glass, wood carving, metalwork, and many other craft products present the objects far more vividly than could photographs, and the renderings are more permanent than any known form of photographic reproduction. Together they form a record of the development of American folk and decorative arts. Thirty-two exhibitions from this vast corpus of more than 17,000 illustrations, are constantly circulated by the Gallery; publishers and industrial designers, too, frequently draw upon this source of Americana.

B. *Music*

The National Gallery of Art is perhaps the only museum in the world with a conductor-composer as part of its staff. On Sunday evenings, except during the summer months, he arranges concerts given in one of the garden courts. These are regularly broadcast and have resulted in a number of recordings which have sold widely. The Gallery concerts are free and have been attended by more than half a million people. Many of the performances are given by the National Gallery Symphony Orchestra, the others by visiting artists.

The concerts were begun during the war, owing to the generosity of Mr Chester Dale, and were continued with funds provided by The A. W. Mellon Educational and Charitable Trust. Recently they have received generous support from the Calouste Gulbenkian Foundation of Lisbon. It is a moving experience to see the crowds, seated and standing, who attend these Sunday evening performances, which have become an important part of the cultural life of Washington.

In the informality of the setting, in the type of small orchestra with its conductor-composer, and in its emphasis on new native compositions, the National Gallery of Art is continuing the eighteenth-century tradition of musical performances under a *Kapellmeister*, which distinguished so many German and Austrian courts.

C. *Science*

The last century and a half has seen an advance in applied science unparalleled in history. We make better steel, build longer bridges, travel in faster vehicles than ever before and live a life completely changed by technological discoveries. Yet there are exceptions to this technical progress. While the tools used to fabricate nearly every commodity have changed, those used to produce art have remained much the same. We paint with pigments not very different and often less lasting than those of the Renaissance, and we apply them in ways generally less durable than the methods of the Old Masters.

Various reasons can be found for this technical backwardness in the fine arts, but the major explanation remains a lack of interest in the kind of full-time research which has made other scientific advances possible. Until recently there has been very little support for serious scientific investigation of artists' materials. In the late 1920s Harvard established at the Fogg Art Museum the first significant laboratory experiments in the United States related to the preservation of art objects. Funds for this program, however, were never abundant and scientific investigation had to be combined with restoration and teaching. Nevertheless, during the last war, when Harvard found it necessary to curtail work in the Fogg laboratory, American museums suffered a severe loss.

Twelve years ago the National Gallery of Art received a grant for research in artists' materials. These funds, provided by the Old Dominion and Avalon Foundations, have made possible a continuation of the work begun at the Fogg Museum. The Gallery's program, however, differs in a significant way from the Harvard program. The scientists have no teaching or restoration responsibilities, and consequently their investigations can proceed without interruptions

54

of this nature. The project is located at the Mellon Institute in Pittsburgh. This immense center for scientific investigation, one of the best-equipped laboratories in the world, offers important advantages. Not only are the most modern tools available, equipment often rare and costly, but scientists working on artists' materials have an opportunity for discussing their research with scores of other scientists doing related work.

It was decided when the National Gallery program began that it would be more practicable to take a chemist and make him aware of the problems of restoration rather than to take a restorer and teach him chemistry. The National Gallery of Art representative at the Mellon Institute, a distinguished chemist, has become familiar with the difficulties confronting museums in preserving paintings. He in turn has trained his assistants. He has worked closely not only with restorers at the National Gallery of Art but also with those in other museums in the United States and abroad.

In the course of his research he has been able to contribute to the solution of certain problems of restoration. To discuss only one, there has been an epidemic of 'whitening' of repaint which has broken out in recent years in many galleries of Europe and the United States. Bluish white areas suddenly began to appear on paintings, like a rash. These always occurred in repainted places which were, on the whole, light in tone. Such areas, of course, had previously matched the surrounding color. After a thorough investigation it has been discovered that certain restorers had been using mixtures of zinc white, colored pigment, and dammar varnish when they retouch. Occasionally, a form of photochemically active titanium white was also detected. The effect of light on this mixture of white pigment and varnish caused the repaint to deteriorate and take on a whitish appearance. The discovery has been widely publicized among restorers, and it is to be hoped that in the future they will avoid this combination of materials.

Though other practical problems of this nature have been solved, the first ten years of the National Gallery of Art's program has been devoted principally to a fundamental study of picture varnish and related types of spirit varnishes. Every oil painting is varnished sooner or later, and this surface coating has always presented a problem. Until recently natural varnishes, dammar and mastic principally, have been used to protect paintings and to give them a certain radiance and luster; but dammar, mastic, and all natural resins have a common flaw: after roughly twenty years they invariably yellow, and this yellowing increases until it destroys chromatic brilliance. Discolored varnish is one of the principal reasons paintings are being repeatedly cleaned. We know that the solvents used in such cleaning are often dangerous and that, even with the most careful handling, they may affect the paint, though to what extent still requires investigation. Some synthetic varnishes, which do not yellow and therefore remain permanently translucent, have been developed. Their manufacturers claim for them all the virtues and none of the defects of natural varnishes. At the Mellon Institute these synthetic materials have been analyzed, new ones have been formulated, and virtually all natural and synthetic resins have been evaluated. This stage of the Gallery's research program has resulted in a definitive publication on spirit varnishes. Now restorers can for the first time use these new varnishes with scientific knowledge of their ingredients, their merits, demerits, and capabilities.

Because of skylights which admit daylight, there has arisen a new problem which we are only beginning to recognize. It is the fading of oil and tempera paintings. Museum directors and curators have always worried about the fading of textiles, prints, drawings, and watercolors; but pictures painted in tempera or oil were deemed on the whole impervious to the destructive effects of light. We now find that this is not the case.

It is luck, to some extent, that our Old Masters are still as brilliant in color as they are. Most paintings in the past were intended for dimly lit churches and dark palaces. In the nineteenth century, for the first time, we placed these panels and canvases in galleries with skylights, where the natural illumination reaching the walls was often a hundred times as great as the light in the buildings where the paintings originally hung. Until recently the damage which might have been caused by this vast increase in brightness of illumination had been kept to a minimum by varnishes which had in due course turned yellow. In the past, moreover, whenever pictures seemed dull and lusterless, instead of cleaning, as we would do today, the usual procedure was to revarnish. This series of yellow coatings, like layers of yellow glass, provided an effective filter, removing to a great extent the ultra-violet rays, and reducing, with the help of a good deal of dirt, the total amount of light from the rest of the spectrum reaching the pigments themselves. Then came the modern taste for pictures cleaned of their old varnish. The protective coat of yellow dammar or mastic was thus removed along with the dirt; and the pigments, covered with only a colorless, transparent varnish, usually a synthetic resin, were exposed under gallery skylights to illumination as high as 600 foot-candles, as against five or six in the average daylit interior of a palace or church.

The National Gallery of Art's research program is investigating the many types of damage that light can cause. It was demonstrated that the effect of light on fugitive pigments is additive, that the light waves of the whole spectrum are deleterious, though ultra-violet rays are generally the most destructive; and that more pigments than we had realized are fugitive. Experimentation is being pushed to improve ultra-violet filters, which can be used over the skylights of galleries, and possibly, infused into the varnish of the pictures themselves; and other methods of reducing the destructive effect of the invisible radiation in the light are being sought. If this search fails to find satisfactory ways of lessening the damaging power of natural light, museums may be compelled to abandon daylight altogether and resort to artificial illumination. The damaging factor in such illumination can be precisely controlled, but there is frequently a loss of aesthetic pleasure. It is to be hoped that science can offer a suitable solution to the use of natural light.

Similar studies of pigments, supports, varnishes, solvents, adhesives, light, and other problems related to the preservation of works of art are being undertaken in a number of European countries, and the most heartening aspect of this scientific research into the nature of artists' materials is the amount of international cooperation taking place. We are rapidly catching up with technical advances in other fields. In the next ten years it seems likely that restorers will be given new materials as revolutionary and as useful as antibiotics in medicine. For this reason it is the policy of the National Gallery of Art to restrict restoration to work necessary for preservation, and to clean paintings as little as possible consistent with their conservation.

CONCLUSION

During its first twenty years the National Gallery of Art has had a growth which might never have occurred if it had been established a few years later. Coming when it did, it has proved to be a magnet for those last great American collections not already given or promised elsewhere. Thus, for two decades treasures have flowed to Washington at an unprecedented rate. It is difficult to believe that there will ever again be a similar influx of masterpieces to any museum.

The National Gallery of Art holds a unique position in America. As the principal agency of the United States Government in the area of the visual arts, it has been called upon to undertake many of the functions performed elsewhere by Ministries of Fine Arts. These responsibilities have varied from assisting in the designs of stamps and inaugural medals to organizing exhibitions offered by foreign governments. The Gallery's creation thus helped to fill a void in the governmental structure.

Its establishment presented the President and the Congress with the challenge of maintaining a Federal art museum for which there was no real precedent. Until then the government's support of museums was directed mainly to the outstanding departments of science and history at the Smithsonian Institution. But with the acceptance of Mr Mellon's gift the experiment of creating a distinguished National Gallery was undertaken. This book is in some ways a balance sheet of accomplishment.

59

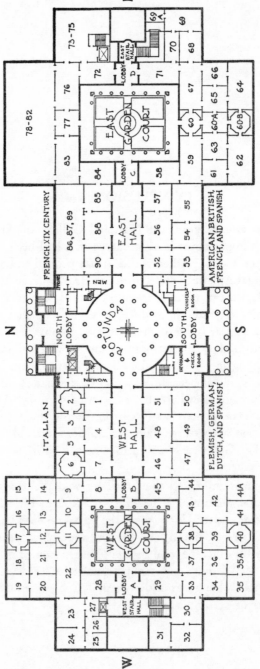

MAIN FLOOR

THE NATIONAL GALLERY OF ART

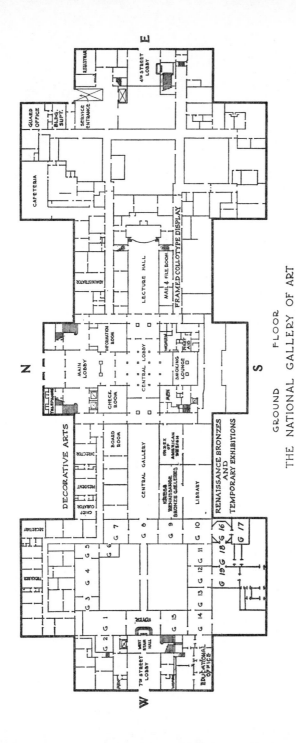

GROUND FLOOR

THE NATIONAL GALLERY OF ART

THE PLATES

BYZANTINE SCHOOL, XIII Century
Enthroned Madonna and Child
Catalogue No. 1048

Wood
Height 51⅝" (131.2 cm.)
Width 30¼" (76.9 cm.)

Panels like this *Madonna and Child* by an anonymous Byzantine artist represent the tradition out of which Western painting developed. 'Monuments of unaging intellect,' such devotional pictures were also considered in the East to be a medium of occult power. Justinian advanced behind a representation of the Virgin to reconquer Italy and much of Africa, and icons were supposed to heal the sick and give sight to the blind.

The style in which such Byzantine icons were painted was the product of two incongruous elements: one, a tradition of forms naturalistically modeled in light and shade, the Byzantine heritage of Roman painting; and opposed to this, the Oriental taste for flat pattern and calligraphic line, a taste derived from those Eastern peoples who rose to power during the last centuries of the Roman Empire. That these components never completely fused is apparent in the icon reproduced. The heads, especially that of the Christ Child, give that illusion of roundness, of three-dimensional form, which is to be found in classical painting. On the other hand, the gold and ivory throne, the flattened bodies of the figures, the emphasis on abstract pattern, all are elements Oriental in origin.

In the drapery especially, one can see the hybrid nature of Byzantine art. The striated folds, which appear purely conventional, are in fact derived from modeling of drapery in classical painting. The areas of gold, with their radiating lines, represent the highlights on the tops of the folds of a cloth woven with gold thread. Those folds, under the influence of Oriental taste, have become stylized until there is only a remote connection with naturalistic light and shade. Here, as in many Byzantine mosaics, the real purpose is to make the figures harmonize with the gold background, and to emphasize, by repetition of accent, a rhythmic sequence that has the same function as a recurrent beat in music.

Byzantine painting flourished throughout Europe until the dawn of the Italian Renaissance. The present panel, which was probably executed in Constantinople about the year 1200, was discovered in a monastery in Spain in the early twentieth century. Doubtless it was left there by some crusading knight or militant ecclesiastic returned from his long pilgrimage to the East. Collections: Church in Calahorra (Aragon), Spain (from an unknown date until first quarter of XX Century); Weissburger, Madrid; Emile Pares, Paris; G. W. Arnold. *Gift of Mrs Otto Kahn*, 1949.

DUCCIO DI BUONINSEGNA (Sienese, active 1278–1319)
THE CALLING OF THE APOSTLES PETER AND ANDREW   Wood
Catalogue No. 252   Height 17¹/₈" (43.5 cm.)
                                                     Width 18¹/₈" (46 cm.)

The greatest single creation of the Byzantine school was painted not in Byzantium but in Siena. The Byzantine tradition culminated in the *Maestà* – *the Virgin in Majesty* – painted for the Cathedral of Siena between 1308 and 1311 by Duccio di Buoninsegna. This altarpiece is a compendium of all that men had learned during a thousand years about the craft of painting. Within the Byzantine style there is no more skillful use of line, pattern, and composition, no finer example of dramatic power and significant characterization.

Duccio's altarpiece was not only the most perfect expression of medieval painting, it also contained the seeds of future development. In *The Calling of the Apostles Peter and Andrew,* a panel which once formed part of the predella of the *Maestà,* there is evidence that the hieratic rigidity of the Byzantine style has changed. There is a tender awareness of human life, of its daily activity. The apostles busily netting their fish, and the aquatic life itself, open new vistas in art. This rudimentary naturalism was stimulated by the growing popularity of the Franciscan interest in nature. But the figure of Christ has still the austerity of Byzantine art. The edge of His robe is still touched with gold which, like a flash of lightning, sets Him apart from common humanity. When the *Maestà* was completed, the Sienese realized that their altarpiece was, of its type, the supreme masterpiece of the age. A great procession was formed to carry it in triumph to the high altar of the Cathedral, and a whole day was devoted to prayers and hymns to the Virgin. Duccio's masterwork, still almost intact, has remained the principal treasure of Siena. Eight panels, however, became separated from the rest and two of these, the one reproduced on the opposite page and a scene of the Nativity (page 257), are now in the National Gallery of Art. Collections: Cathedral of Siena; Robert H. and Evelyn Benson, London; Clarence H. Mackay, Roslyn, New York. *Samuel H. Kress Collection,* 1934. Painted between 1308 and 1311.

GIOTTO (Florentine, 1266–1336)
MADONNA AND CHILD   Wood
Catalogue No. 367   Height 33⅝" (85.5 cm.)
                                          Width 24⅜" (62 cm.)

Duccio sums up the past; Giotto foretells the future. Both artists typify
the spirit of the cities in which they lived. Siena was conservative, sophisticated, over-refined; Florence was experimental, vigorous, dynamic. Duccio's
style was the flowering of an ancient tradition; but Giotto's paintings, based on study of the human form and stimulated by intellectual
curiosity, tore apart the formulas of the immediate past. Duccio developed
the Eastern elements of Byzantine art, line, pattern, and composition on
a flat plane. Giotto emphasized instead, form, mass, and volume—the
almost forgotten tradition of classical painting.

To appreciate the difference between these two approaches to painting,
compare the figures in *The Calling of the Apostles Peter and Andrew* by
Duccio, on the preceding page, and the figures of the *Madonna and Child*
by Giotto. One feels intuitively something like a difference in specific
gravity, as though Duccio's figures were made of aluminium and Giotto's
of lead. It was Giotto's passion for solidity that determined the appearance of his figures, that caused him to depict large-boned, massive models.
He willingly sacrificed superficial physical beauty to convey more intensely physical existence. This *Madonna and Child,* which may once have
formed part of the celebrated polyptych painted by Giotto for the Badia
in Florence, is typical. It seems carved from a monolith as solid as a piece
of granite. Every device is used to enhance the feeling of substance. Look,
for instance, at the powerful rendering of the hands, the thickness and
roundness of the fingers, the sense of existence conveyed by the manner in
which the Christ Child grasps His Mother's forefinger.

Here Giotto has given us the essential quality of significant Florentine
painting. Two hundred years later Leonardo da Vinci was to define this
quality in the following words: 'The first object of the painter is to make
a flat plane appear as a body in relief and projecting from that plane.'
In Giotto's work this suggestion of relief is rendered with a power that
has never been surpassed. Collections: Edouard de Max, Paris; Henry
Goldman, New York. *Samuel H. Kress Collection,* 1937. Painted c.1320.

MASACCIO (Florentine, 1401–1427/28)
PROFILE PORTRAIT OF A YOUNG MAN   Wood
Catalogue No. 14   Height 16⅝" (42 cm.)
                                          Width 12¾" (32 cm.)

Giotto's attainment of the suggestion of sculptural form died with him. His followers lost sight of his objective. They were seduced by a love of accessories, by a desire to represent rich stuffs for their own richness, by graceful gestures for their own grace. Thus they forgot form for pattern. This attractive heresy culminated in the so-called International Style, which at the end of the fourteenth century flourished everywhere.

At the beginning of the fifteenth century, however, Florentine artists were recalled to the true faith, so to speak, by a fanatic for form, Tommaso di Ser Giovanni Guidi, called Masaccio. His panel paintings are extremely rare. Berenson lists only fourteen. Though it is difficult to attribute with complete conviction profile portraits of the fifteenth century, the qualities of sculptural form which distinguish this painting support Berenson's ascription of the panel to Masaccio. Note its subtle qualities of relief achieved by delicate transitions of value from light to shade, which model the lid of the eye, the concavity under the jaw, and the plastic convolutions of the ear.

Rendering three-dimensional form with a new flexibility, Masaccio adapted it to new purposes. The discovery in the fifteenth century of classical coins and busts stimulated a desire for portraiture and the perpetuation of personality which it can give. Masaccio endowed his sitters with this immortality. Like Shakespeare, he could assert:

> 'So long as men can breathe, or eyes can see
> So long lives this, and this gives life to thee.'

Collections: Artaud de Montor, Paris. *Mellon Collection,* 1937. Painted c. 1425.

SASSETTA (Sienese, active 1423–1450)
THE MEETING OF ST ANTHONY AND ST PAUL   Wood
Catalogue No. 404   Height 18³/₄" (47.5 cm.)
                                                      Width 13⁵/₈" (34.5 cm.)

In the early decades of the fifteenth century the late Gothic style flowered
in such enchanting paintings as this, *The Meeting of St Anthony and St
Paul* by Sassetta. In spite of medieval characteristics such as the high
horizon line and the method of continuous narration whereby three scenes
from the life of the saint are shown at once, Sassetta reveals a sensitive observation of nature as advanced as any painter of his age. The landscape
with its arid hills, its groves of dark, dense foliage is the distilled essence
of the *Senese*, of that beautiful region of Tuscany near Siena where Sassetta
lived and worked.

Sassetta was one of the most gifted of narrative painters. In a series of
predella panels, four of which are in the National Gallery of Art (Catalogue Nos. 817, 818, 1152), he has told, more poetically than any other
artist, the legend of St Anthony Abbot. The panel reproduced, the sixth
of the series, tells of the visit of St Anthony to St Paul. The tradition is
that St Anthony, having a vision of a fellow hermit, St Paul, who had
attained great sanctity, decided to pay him a visit. In the upper left-hand
corner, staff in hand, St Anthony sets out on his journey. On his way he
meets a centaur, a symbol of the gods of paganism, fast vanishing from
the Christian world. The centaur, holding a palm branch, beats on his
breast as a sign of his penitence, and receives a blessing – an indication
of the conversion to Christianity of the ancient divinities of the woods.

At the bottom of the picture the two old men at last find each other.
Their deep emotion is beautifully suggested by their tender embrace. As
they incline their bodies one toward the other their halos overlap, and
the two figures form a pyramid whose shape is echoed in the opening of
the cave and in the barren hill beyond. The intensity of feeling Sassetta
conveys gives this small panel an impressive grandeur, making it one of
the noblest creations of Sienese painting. Collections: G. E. H. Vernon;
Thomas Wentworth Beaumont; Viscount Allendale, London. *Samuel H.
Kress Collection*, 1938. Painted c. 1445.

QVANTVM·HOMINI·FAS·EST·MIRA·LICET·ASSEQVAR·ARTE
NIL·AGO·MORTALIS·EMVLOR·ARTE·DEOS·

NEROCCIO DE' LANDI (Sienese, 1446–1500)
PORTRAIT OF A LADY   Wood
Catalogue No. 643   Height 18³/₈″ (46.5 cm.)
                         Width 12″ (30.5 cm.)

Curiously enough, in Siena, in contrast to Florence and the Central Italian cities, scarcely any portraits were produced in the fifteenth century. Therefore the *Portrait of a Lady* in the Widener Collection is of inestimable value. It bears an important inscription, which in translation reads, 'Although by wondrous dexterity I may reach the summit of human achievement, yet am I doomed to failure. A mortal, I am pitting my art against that of the gods.' On one side of the inscription are the letters NER. which have generally been considered an abbreviation of Neroccio. On the other side are the initials A. P., which Berenson believed probably stood for Alessandra Piccolomini, a Sienese heiress and grandniece of Pius II, who married the hereditary governor of Aquila, a city of the Abruzzi. The frame, which must be contemporary with the picture, is ornamented with a series of beaks, perhaps as Berenson thought a reference to *aquila*, the Italian word for eagle, though Gertrude Coor, who identifies the sitter differently, connects them with the heraldic device of the Bandini family.

Confronted by an example of portraiture of such jewel-like beauty, we are astonished to realize that, not only is it the single portrait by Neroccio, but also that it is almost the only portrait in Sienese art of the fifteenth century. Why did a city, so richly dowered with artists as was Siena, even in the Quattrocento, produce virtually no portraits? Possibly the inscription hints at the reason: '...A mortal, I am pitting my art against that of the gods.' Was there a superstition in Siena, the most superstitious of Italian cities, that there was something unlucky in portraiture? If so, it may have been encouraged by the fate of the beautiful sitter of this portrait, assuming Berenson's identification to be correct. Only a short time after she was painted by Neroccio, her husband, in Berenson's words, 'fell into disgrace and had to run for his life, settling down in the Marches at Recanati where his wife died.' Collection: *Widener Collection,* 1942. Painted c. 1490.

FRA ANGELICO and FRA FILIPPO LIPPI
(Florentine, 1387–1455 and c. 1406–1469)

THE ADORATION OF THE MAGI   Wood

Catalogue No. 1085   Diameter 54″ (137.2 cm.)

This tondo ranks among the greatest Florentine paintings in the world. It is a climax of beauty, a summary in itself of the whole evolution of the Italian schools of painting in the first half of the fifteenth century. For it stands at a crossroad of art. The old style, the gay, colorful, fairy tale painting of the Middle Ages, is ending in an outburst of splendor; and the new style, scientific in observation, studious in anatomy and perspective, realistic in its portrayal of life, is beginning its long development. Two harbingers of the future are the row of naked youths who watch the procession – an early indication of that preoccupation with human anatomy, which was to obsess Italian artists until it reached its climax in Michelangelo and the Sistine Chapel – and the scene in the stable, which foretells the flowering of genre painting at a still later date. It is interesting to note the degree to which Florentine style for the next fifty years fell under the spell of the two monks who collaborated on this *Adoration of the Magi*. It is almost as though the Kress Collection tondo seeded a whole garden of art.

Berenson was the first to indicate the probable collaboration of two artists on this panel, concluding that it was probably left unfinished when Fra Angelico departed for Rome in 1445. Though he subsequently came to agree with most critics that the painting was largely by Fra Filippo Lippi, the influence of Fra Angelico is everywhere apparent, and in some cases his touch can be discerned. The tondo has been connected with an entry in the Medici inventory of 1492 made after the death of Lorenzo the Magnificent, which reads: 'A tondo with its golden frame representing the Madonna and Our Lord and the Magi offering gifts, from the hand of Fra Giovanni [Fra Angelico] worth 100 florins.' This was the highest price in the inventory. Collections: Probably Guicciardini Palace, Florence; probably M. Dubois, Florence; William Coningham, London; Alexander Barker, London; Cook, Doughty House, Richmond, Surrey. *Samuel H. Kress Collection,* 1947. Painted probably c. 1445.

DOMENCIO VENEZIANO (Florentine, c. 1400–1461)

ST JOHN IN THE DESERT — Wood

Catalogue No. 715

Height 11¹/₈" (28.5 cm.)

Width 12³/₄" (32.5 cm.)

The Renaissance artist was confronted with the problem of paganism and Christianity. How could he bring into harmony the classical world he was learning to love, as he came to know it, and the Christian doctrines and traditions, which were his immediate heritage? He rarely solved this problem, rarely achieved complete reconciliation. When, however, he managed to bring the two forces into perfect balance, as they are in this painting by Domenico Veneziano, there is a magic calm, a breathless moment, in which the underlying tensions of Renaissance art are miraculously resolved.

Few pictures present so perfectly the essence of the Quattrocento – the youthful spirit of a new world emerging from the shadows of the Middle Ages into the cold beauty of the dawning Renaissance. St John is a nude athlete with a body that might have been carved by Polycleitus; but above his head appears a golden halo, the emblem of his sanctity. The panel has always been thought to represent, in a virtually unique form, the moment when St John put aside his worldly clothes and assumed the rough garb of the wilderness. But is there also a second meaning, another interpretation more subtle, more in keeping with the classical spirit which permeates the picture? Is this youth putting aside instead the drab clothes of his mortal body and reaching for the iridescent garments of a spiritual realm he is about to enter? As the panel was a part of an altarpiece now in the Uffizi, undoubtedly the usual Christian story of St John donning his hair shirt was the interpretation intended for the public. But there is throughout the picture an evocative fancy, a suggestion of some half-disclosed symbolism, perhaps some Neoplatonic theory of the progress of the soul, which makes this second and quite different meaning not impossible.

Regardless of iconography, this panel and a few other works by Domenico Veneziano must have had a revolutionary effect on the painting of their day. Here for the first time we find a landscape filled with sparkling air, like a high plateau swept clean with cool winds. To be able to convey the mood of a particular place was new in art, and it has remained rare. Collections: Santa Lucia dei Magnoli, Florence; Bernard Berenson, Florence; Carl W. Hamilton, New York. *Samuel H. Kress Collection*, 1942. Painted c. 1445. Another panel, *St Francis Receiving the Stigmata* (page 298), from the same predella is in the National Gallery of Art.

ANDREA DEL CASTAGNO (Florentine, c. 1420–1457)

THE YOUTHFUL DAVID

Catalogue No. 604

Leather

Height 45¹/₂″ (115.5 cm.)

Width 30¹/₄″ (77 cm.)

One of the most vivid tales in Vasari's *Lives of the Painters* is the description of the brutal murder of Domenico Veneziano by his pupil Andrea del Castagno. We now know that Vasari's account is fictitious, for Domenico outlived his supposed murderer; but if a man's personality is reflected in his creations, then Vasari's characterization of Castagno is true. Truculence, bravado, a brutal power, these are the qualities that emanate from his work.

In his interpretation of the triumphant David, he is less aggressive, less savage than one would expect, but he displays, nevertheless, his power to overwhelm us with the sheer impact of emotion. The intense vitality of this heroic youth, vibrant with energy, anticipates the romanticism of Géricault and Delacroix.

David is a symbolic figure, the ideal warrior, hard, resolute, conscious of his power, but conscious at the same time of its tragic implications. The head of the slain Goliath already lies at his feet. To the modern spectator this may seem an inconsistency in the sequence of events, but it did not disturb Castagno's contemporaries, for the picture is symbolic. It is not the representation of a historic occurrence. Consequently the act and the result of the act are shown simultaneously. For the meaning of the scene, the triumph of freedom over tyranny, could best be expressed this way.

The painting is on a leather shield and was probably carried in the processions which preceded the jousts, or tournaments, popular in the fifteenth century. Other ornamental shields exist, though they are rare, but this example is the only one by a great master that has survived. Collections: Drury-Lowe, Locko Park, England. *Widener Collection,* 1942. Painted c. 1450.

BOTTICELLI (Florentine, 1444–1510)
THE ADORATION OF THE MAGI   Wood
Catalogue No. 22   Height 27⅝″ (71 cm.)
                                                  Width 41″ (103.5 cm.)

With this *Adoration of the Magi* we reach the last quarter of the fifteenth
century and the reign of Lorenzo de' Medici. Florence had become a center
of Greek studies, Neoplatonism almost a religion. Refinement, a fastidious
sensibility, a mood of poetic reverie had come into fashion. It was a time
when pageants and ceremonials were popular and families took pride in
having themselves portrayed as the principal actors in the dramas of
Christianity. In the present painting, which Botticelli probably executed
during his sojourn in Rome while he was working in the Sistine Chapel,
the portraits have never been identified in spite of their incisive charac-
terizations.

But the wonder of this *Adoration* does not consist so much in these
portrait studies as in the subtle disposition of the figures, in their vibrant
movement, and their poetic setting. Amid the ruins of the classical world,
symbolized by fragments of ancient architecture, the new order of Christianity is born. From the calmness of the central group, from the mystical
yet human serenity of the Madonna and Child, movement radiates in
waves of increasing activity through the gestures of awe and of prayer of
the onlookers, and reaches a climax in the youthful grooms on the far right.

Beyond this human activity stretches a landscape suggestive of the serene
spaces of the *Campagna*. It is impossible to let the eye travel into the tranquil beauty of this countryside without some relief of the spirit, some sense
of refreshment and calm. The breath, serenity, and restraint which are so
conspicuous in this *Adoration* disappeared shortly thereafter from Botticelli's
work. With the exile of the Medici he came under the spell of Savonarola
and his last years were overclouded by the feverish visions of the Do-
minican reformer. Collections: Purchased in Rome by the engraver, Peralli,
it was acquired in 1808 for the Hermitage Gallery, Leningrad, by Czar
Alexander I. *Mellon Collection*, 1937. Painted c. 1481–1482.

BOTTICELLI (Florentine, 1444–1510)
GIULIANO DE' MEDICI   Wood
Catalogue No. 1135   Height 29³/₄" (75.6 cm.)
                                             Width 20⁵/₈" (52.6 cm.)

In looking at portraits one is reminded of something Robert Louis Stevenson once said about Sir Henry Raeburn's work: 'These portraits are racier than many anecdotes and more complete than many a volume of sententious memoirs.' The statement is certainly applicable to Botticelli's portrait of Giuliano de' Medici, the younger brother of Lorenzo the Magnificent. Giuliano was himself a favorite of that circle of poets, artists, and scholars who wrote one of the most glorious pages in the history of Western culture.

All Italy was shocked in 1478 when the twenty-five-year-old prince was stabbed to death in the Cathedral of Florence. This may well have been the most sacrilegious murder ever committed, for the conspirators' signal for the onslaught was the bell rung at the elevation of the Host; they knew that at that moment all would bow their heads in reverence. Lorenzo de' Medici was wounded in the neck and escaped, but Giuliano died at the foot of the high altar.

Whether Botticelli painted his friend posthumously or shortly before the murder is disputed. Nor can we be sure of the meaning of the turtle dove perching on a dead branch on the window sill. The symbolism itself is clear: the widowed turtle dove remains faithful to its mate and will alight only on a blighted tree. But does the symbolism apply to Giuliano's passionate devotion to Simonetta Vespucci, one of the most beautiful of all Florentine ladies, who had died two years earlier? Or is it a symbol of Lorenzo's ceaseless mourning for his brother? Collection: *Samuel H. Kress Collection*, 1949. Painted c. 1476.

PIERO DI COSIMO (Florentine, 1462–c. 1521)　　　　Wood
THE VISITATION AND TWO SAINTS　　　　Height 72½" (184 cm.)
Catalogue No. 454　　　　Width 74¼" (189 cm.)

The tales of personal eccentricities told by early biographers of Piero di
Cosimo find support in the whimsical air of his allegorical and mythological paintings, in the enigmatic expressions of some of his religious figures,
and in the fantastic eruptions in his landscape backgrounds. Yet in spite of
his originality, Piero was one of the most eclectic of the great Florentine
painters.

He seems to have been under the spell of Filippino Lippi when he painted
this large altarpiece of the *Visitation* for a family chapel in the church of
Santo Spirito, Florence. The group of the Virgin and St Elizabeth, for which
a drawing by Piero is still preserved in the Uffizi, recalls Filippino's
recherché poses and gestures and his graceful design of thin, gold-trimmed
veils. There may be Northern influence in the buildings that form back-

Continued on page 100

PIETRO PERUGINO (Umbrian, c. 1445–1523)
THE CRUCIFIXION WITH THE VIRGIN, ST JOHN,
ST JEROME, AND ST MARY MAGDALEN　　Transferred from wood to canvas
Catalogue No. 27　　　　Center: Height 39⅞" (101.5 cm.)
　　　　　　　　　　　　　　　　Width 22¼" (56.5 cm.)
　　　　　　　　　　　　Sides: Height 37½" (95 cm.)
　　　　　　　　　　　　　　　　Width 12" (30.5 cm.)

In his meditation on Good Friday and in his *Journal intime*, Henri-Frédéric
Amiel has written, 'From a long contemplation of this theme – the agony
of the Just, peace in the midst of agony, and glory in such peace – mankind
came to understand that a new religion had been born, that is, a new way
of explaining life and of understanding suffering . . .'

Perugino's paintings create to a degree rare in art a mood of tranquil
veneration, in which such religious truths appear self-evident or demon-
strable. It is surprising therefore to learn from Vasari that Perugino was a
person of little religion and disbelieved in the immortality of the soul.

The present triptych was formerly ascribed to Perugino's pupil, Raphael,
but as we know that it was given to the Church of San Domenico at

Continued on page 99

86

ERCOLE ROBERTI (Ferrarese, c. 1456–1496)   Wood
GINEVRA BENTIVOGLIO   Height 21¹/₈″ (54 cm.)
Catalogue No. 331   Width 15¹/₄″ (39 cm.)

In the second half of the fifteenth century a current of Florentine influence swept over the rest of Italy. It spread through Tuscany to Arezzo, Borgo San Sepolcro, and Urbino where Piero della Francesca was creating his triumphant and impersonal beauty. It flooded Padua, where Donatello, Filippo Lippi, and Paolo Uccello all worked at various times. From Padua it flowed to the other cities of the Veneto, of Emilia, and of Lombardy. Everywhere it appeared, it swept aside the indigenous Gothic style.

What happened in Ferrara, the capital of the Este dominions, is typical. Piero della Francesca brought there the recent discoveries in the rendering of light and in the suggestion of atmosphere, which he had learned from Domenico Veneziano. These innovations he passed on to Ercole Roberti, and they appear in Roberti's double portrait of Giovanni II Bentivoglio (page 301) and his wife Ginevra. Collections: Louis Charles Timbal; Gustave Dreyfus, Paris. *Samuel H. Kress Collection*, 1936. Painted c. 1480.

GIOVANNI BELLINI (Venetian, c. 1430–1516)   Wood
PORTRAIT OF A CONDOTTIERE   Height 19¹/₄″ (49 cm.)
Catalogue No. 335   Width 13⁷/₈″ (35 cm.)

When this portrait was painted around 1480, Giovanni Bellini, who lived to be over eighty, was the acknowledged leader of the Venetian school of painting. As Vasari, writing in the sixteenth century, said, 'Since he had the habit of painting portraits from life, he made it the fashion in that city for anyone of prominence to be portrayed by him or someone else.' Not only did Giovanni Bellini popularize portraiture in Venice, he was one of the first to start the vogue for a three-quarter view of the sitter, replacing the older, profile type exemplified by Ercole Roberti's portrait of Ginevra Bentivoglio (page 89). This new way of posing the sitter was probably introduced into Italy by artists from Flanders, who also brought with them the technique of painting in oil. Giovanni Bellini, always alert to innovations, recognized that the three-quarter view permitted better characterization and that the use of oil instead of tempera allowed a greater refinement of modeling. Collections: Sir Abraham Hume. *Samuel H. Kress Collection*, 1936. Painted c. 1480.

ANDREA MANTEGNA (Paduan, 1431–1506)
JUDITH AND HOLOFERNES   Wood
Catalogue No. 638   Height 11⅞″ (30 cm.)
                                               Width 7⅛″ (18 cm.)

The search for actuality and the discovery of archaeology molded fifteenth-century Italian painting. Padua, where Mantegna was born, was a center of antiquarianism. Even in a scene from the Old Testament, Judith decapitating Holofernes, we find the Jewish drama transformed into a Greek tragedy. Thus the actors, in spite of the gruesomeness of the event, are as impersonal as the sculptured figures of the Parthenon. Judith turns away from her bloody prize with a look of calm detachment; she accepts impassively her predestined triumph. The stone-colored panel seems chiseled rather than painted, like an enlarged cameo which has survived from the ancient world.

Such classicism appealed strongly to seventeenth-century taste, especially in England. The first recorded owner of this panel was Charles I, who believed it to be by Raphael. Later he exchanged it with the Earl of Pembroke for paintings by Bellini and Parmigianino. Thus it escaped one of the tragic consequences of Cromwell's Revolution, the dispersal of the Royal Collection. It remained in England instead, a part of the famous Pembroke Collection at Wilton House until brought to America by Mr P. A. B. Widener. The subject of Judith and Holofernes was treated several times by Mantegna and his school. Among the drawings of this scene are one in the Uffizi, Florence (dated 1491), and one in the Samuel H. Kress Collection, National Gallery of Art (No. 289). A grisaille of almost identical dimensions, showing the same subject, with the composition in reverse, is in the National Gallery, Dublin. Judith, the unscrupulous murderer of tyrants, was the most popular heroine of the Renaissance. Collections: King Charles I of England; Pembroke Collection, Wilton House. *Widener Collection*, 1942. Painted c. 1495.

JAN VAN EYCK (Flemish, 1380/1400–1441)

THE ANNUNCIATION   Transferred from wood to canvas

Catalogue No. 39   Height 36¹/₂″ (93 cm.)

Width 14³/₈″ (36.5 cm.)

In many ways the founder of all Northern painting was Jan van Eyck, who died in Bruges in 1441. He is traditionally considered the discoverer of oil painting – using linseed oil as the medium for color instead of the Italian technique of tempera which utilized egg as the medium. This made possible a new flexibility and delicacy of handling.

Whether or not van Eyck actually did discover oil painting may be debated, but certainly he was the first to achieve a naturalistic rendering of interior space, or in less technical terms, the effect of looking through an open window or door into a room. It is this new power of representation which is van Eyck's most salient characteristic. Note his masterful suggestion of atmosphere through subtle gradations of light, and his supreme skill in the definition of detail. Contrast the barely visible frescoes at the top of the dimly-lit walls of the church, painted with an impalpable delicacy and the hard microscopic clarity of the jewels on the angel's robes. No artist has ever had a greater range of visual effects. *The Annunciation,* however, is more than a record of new technical attainment; it is a masterpiece of Christian symbolism. It expounds the significance of the Annunciation, the momentous event in history which divides the Era of Law from the Era of Grace, the Dispensation of the Old Testament from the New. The dark upper part of the church with its single window on which is depicted Jehovah, the Lord of the Old Testament, is contrasted with the lower half illumined by three windows, symbolic of the Trinity, through which shines the Light of the World. The angel addresses Our Lady with the words *Ave Gratia Plena* to which She answers *Ecce Ancilla Domini,* the words reversed and inverted so they can be read by the Holy Ghost, descending in rays of light.

The building cannot be identified with an existing church, but it suggests the late Romanesque style of Maastricht and Tournai. It would seem as though van Eyck designed this building in an architectural style which had not been practiced for several centuries, perhaps the first example of 'revivalism' in architecture. Collections: Recorded as having been ordered by Philip the Good, Duke of Burgundy, for a church in Dijon; William II, King of the Netherlands; Hermitage Gallery, Leningrad. *Mellon Collection,* 1937. Painted c. 1425/30.

PETRUS CHRISTUS (Flemish, c. 1410–1472/73)

THE NATIVITY

Catalogue No. 40

Wood

Height 51¼″ (130 cm.)
Width 38¼″ (97 cm.)

Glimpses of landscape in Flemish painting are always rewarding. The background of the Petrus Christus *Nativity* shows how pleasant the countryside must have been in the fifteenth century. The town walls kept building within bounds. There were no suburbs. One stepped from the gate of the city directly into meadowland. Nothing could seem closer to an earthly paradise than the world the Flemish artists portrayed. Fortunately, the smells, the dirt, the lack of sanitation of urban life in the Middle Ages had no place in the visual arts.

Painters were not paid to represent the facts of life. Theirs was a different task – to portray the facts of religion. In the foreground of his painting Petrus Christus tells us the story of Man's Fall and Redemption; Adam and Eve stand on columns supported on the backs of stooped figures, symbolizing mankind burdened with Original Sin. Above on the arch are scenes showing the Expulsion from Eden, Cain slaying Abel, and other episodes from the Old Testament. In the spandrels are two battling figures, mankind in hopeless conflict and enmity as a consequence of sin.

These simulated sculpture groups give the historical reason for the action in the center where Mary and Joseph, accompanied by angels, worship the Redeemer. This moment of dramatic stillness, so portentous for mankind, must often have been acted out in a similar way in mystery plays, even to the wooden shoes of St Joseph which lend a sense of actuality to the scene. In the middle distance are four spectators, symbols of humanity, for whose Redemption the Incarnation has taken place. Confronted by a vision of compelling eloquence their indifference, so characteristic of mankind, remains tragically unchanged. Collections: Prince Manuel Yturbe, Madrid; Duchess of Parcent, Madrid. *Mellon Collection*, 1937. Painted c. 1445–46, according to Tolnay; somewhat later, according to J. Held.

ROGIER VAN DER WEYDEN (Flemish, 1399/1400–1464)
PORTRAIT OF A LADY   Wood
Catalogue No. 44   Width 10³/₄″ (0.27 cm.)
                                                    Height 14¹/₂″ (0.37 cm.)

Among the hundreds of portraits at the National Gallery of Art there is
one as beautiful as it is baffling. It is the portrait by Rogier van der
Weyden of a young lady tentatively identified as a famous heiress of the
fifteenth century, Marie de Valengin, daughter of Philip the Good, Duke
of Burgundy. The painting's attraction is twofold: its excellent preservation
and the fascination of the lady who sat for it. As is usual with Flemish
pictures of this period, it is painted on a piece of wood overlaid with white
gesso. On this prepared panel the figure was first painted in monochrome,
and the underpainting then covered with thin glazes of colored oil. With
this newly discovered oil technique the artist was able to render the most
subtle gradations of light, especially noticeable in passages such as the
transparent wimple. With age such Flemish panels have acquired a web
of minute cracks, a surface as beautiful in its way as the surface of old
porcelain.

Though the precision of Flemish painting was suited to the firm structure
and sharp contours of Marie de Valengin's features, if the sitter is she, the
clarity of this style only stresses her somewhat eccentric appearance, and
underlines the conflicting tendencies of her personality.

The first impression is of her preoccupation. Her stare, so oblivious of
the spectator, is like a challenging withdrawal; she looks out from a citadel
of secrecy. Then one notices her meager body made to appear still thinner
by her silken girdle, and afterward her high, intellectual forehead, its
domelike appearance exaggerated by its diaphanous covering. All this is
psychologically consistent, every detail indicative of a contemplative, somewhat ascetic nature. But this is only one aspect of her character. There is
another side, eagerly sensuous and fiercely passionate. It is shown by the
thick underlip and the full mouth. Thus the actions of this Burgundian
princess must always have been unpredictable, always determined by an
unresolved conflict in her personality. Collections: Duke of Anhalt-Dessau,
Gotisches Haus, Worlitz, and Herzogliches Schloss, Dessau, Germany.
Mellon Collection, 1937. Painted c.1455.

HANS MEMLING (Flemish, c. 1430/35–1494)   Wood
THE PRESENTATION IN THE TEMPLE   Height 23¹/₂″ (59.8 cm.)
Catalogue No. 1389   Width 19″ (48.3 cm.)

The problem of attribution grows complicated when it seems possible that two artists have worked on the same picture. Among the most beautiful and best preserved Flemish Primitives is *The Presentation in the Temple* which the Kress Foundation acquired from the Czernin Collection in Vienna. This panel is now generally ascribed to the youthful Hans Memling, working in the studio of Rogier van der Weyden.

The two enchanting children in the scene look different from Memling's typical portraits, as a Belgian critic, Hulin de Loo, first pointed out. They are more delicately painted and convey a greater sense of form than the other figures. Were they, as Hulin de Loo insists, painted by Rogier van der Weyden, and thus an addition by the old master to his pupil's panel? This seems not unlikely, and X-rays of the picture appear to bear out Hulin de Loo's theory.

In order to convey the teachings of Christian theology in visual terms Hans Memling has employed symbolic devices. The church in which the Presentation of Our Lord takes place is Romanesque on the inside and Gothic on the outside. The change in architectural style indicates the change from the Old to the New Dispensation which will result from the Incarnation. The stained-glass windows in the background illustrate the Fall of Man, whereas the foreground prefigures his Redemption. Thus in one scene the artist symbolically portrays certain basic principles of Christian doctrine. Collections: Count Johann Rudolf Czernin von Chudenitz, Vienna; Czernin Gallery, Vienna. *Samuel H. Kress Collection,* 1955. Painted c. 1463.

Continued from page 86
San Gimignano by Bartolommeo Bartoli, who died in 1497, when Raphael was only fourteen, we can be certain that the attribution was incorrect. The picture is now unanimously ascribed to Perugino. It is one of the greatest treasures acquired by Mr Mellon from the Hermitage Gallery, Leningrad. Collections: Bartolommeo Bartoli; Antonio Moggi; Dr Buzzi; Prince Theodore Galitzin; Galitzin Museum; Hermitage Gallery, Leningrad. *Mellon Collection,* 1937. Painted c. 1485.

GERARD DAVID (Flemish, c. 1460–1523)
THE REST ON THE FLIGHT INTO EGYPT   Wood
Catalogue No. 43   Height 17³/₄" (45 cm.)
                                                    Width 17¹/₂" (44.5 cm.)

Flemish painting is characterized by a curious mixture of observation and
tradition. In this connection the small wicker basket in the foreground of
David's *Rest on the Flight into Egypt* is revealing. It is only natural that
Our Lady should have taken a traveling bag on her journey, and for this
accessory David designed a little reticule which was to prove so popular
that it appears sporadically in other paintings for almost a hundred years.
The scene depicted, a pause on a journey, is one he must often have seen.
In the middle distance, the father, beating chestnuts from a tree, is
gathering food; while in the foreground the mother has already begun to
feed her child. But there is more in this scene than a glimpse of a family
at mealtime. A transcript of actuality is combined with an ancient symbolism. A family pauses to eat, but the food, the grapes, are a sign of the
Eucharist, a prefiguration of the Last Supper and of the suffering which
awaits Our Lord. Early Flemish painting has often a double significance:
as a mirror of everyday life and as a symbol of the life to come.
Collections: Rev. Montague Taylor, London; Rodolphe Kann, Paris; J.
Pierpont Morgan, New York; *Mellon Collection,* 1937. Painted c. 1510.

Continued from page 86

grounds for the supplementary scenes of the Adoration of the Shepherds
and the Slaughter of the Innocents; and the famous Flemish altarpiece
finished in 1475 for the Florentine Medici agent, Tommaso Portinari,
probably persuaded Piero to paint with such realistic detail St Nicholas
and St Anthony seated in the foreground and the remarkable spray of
flowers lying on the floor between them. The representation of a number
of scenes within the picture is a medieval tradition. The Annunciation is
depicted as a church decoration in the right background, and on the left,
around a bend in the fantastic rock formation, the procession of the Magi
is just coming into view. Collections: Chapel of Gino Capponi, Santo
Spirito, Florence; Marchese Gaetano Capponi, Villa Capponi, Legnaia,
Florence; Colonel W. Cornwallis-West, Newlands Manor, Hampshire, England. *Samuel H. Kress Collection,* 1937. Painted c. 1490.

MASTER OF THE ST LUCY LEGEND (Flemish, active 1480–1489)
MARY, QUEEN OF HEAVEN   Wood
Catalogue No. 1096   Height 85" (215.9 cm.)
                                          Width 73" (185.4 cm.)

The panel reproduced, which is exceptionally large, is outstanding among Flemish paintings both in preservation and color. It is interesting therefore that it should have been executed with an unusual technique. Whereas nearly all Flemish paintings have a coat of gesso made of white chalk and glue covering the wood, in this case the paint is laid directly on the panel. One is reminded that the altar by Nuno Gonçalves in Lisbon, painted in the same technique, is also unusual in scale and perfectly preserved. It is possible that this variation from the normal Flemish method represented an improvement in the durability of large panel paintings, and, in any case, it was a technique which must have been simpler to handle.

The instruments represented are of considerable significance in the history of music. According to the eminent musicologist, Emmanuel Winternitz, 'All the instruments are contemporary with the painting and depicted with the greatest exactness as if the artist had transplanted into Heaven a musical performance of his own time. Equally precise is the rendering of the finger positions, the holding of the bow, etc. Also, the organization of the two orchestras and their quantitative relation to small vocal groups is by no means fanciful; it is quite in line with contemporary practice. The music sheets are clearly legible.' The St Lucy Master also used color in a musical way, for the angels' robes, like chromatic chords, form together a polyphonic harmony of hues. Though apparently trained in Flanders, this artist was probably active in Spain, as the panel came from a convent near Burgos. Collections: Convent near Burgos, Spain. *Samuel H. Kress Collection,* 1949. Painted c.1485.

MASTER OF ST GILLES (Franco-Flemish, c. 1500)
THE BAPTISM OF CLOVIS   Wood
Catalogue No. 1098   Height 24¹/₄″ (61.6 cm.)
                                             Width 18³/₈″ (46.7 cm.)

The Flemish technique of painting spread over northern Europe and Spain. *The Baptism of Clovis* is the work of a Flemish artist, a pupil perhaps of Hugo van der Goes, who spent much of his life in France. The scene depicted is described thus by Gibbon: 'The important ceremony was performed in the cathedral of Rheims, with every circumstance of magnificence and solemnity that could impress an awful sense of religion on the minds of its rude proselytes. The new Constantine was immediately baptized, with three thousand of his warlike subjects; and their example was imitated by the remainder of the *gentle Barbarians,* who, in obedience to the victorious prelate, adored the cross which they had burnt, and burnt the idols which they had formerly adored.'

In the painting reproduced the scene is shown taking place in Sainte-Chapelle in Paris instead of at Rheims. The upper church is represented as though it were on the ground level. The statue and the porch of Sainte-Chapelle are still visible today, but the Palais de Justice to be seen on the left has vanished. This picture and a companionpiece (page 305) also in the National Gallery of Art, painted about the time America was discovered, are, except for manuscript illumination, the earliest accurate views of the city of Paris. Thus, apart from the beauty of the paintings, they are archaeological documents of outstanding significance. Collections: Comte Alexandre de Lestang-Parade, Aix-en-Provence; Alexandre and Melchior Lestang-Parade; Baron E. de Beurnonville; M. Watil, Paris. *Samuel H. Kress Collection,* 1946. Painted c. 1500.

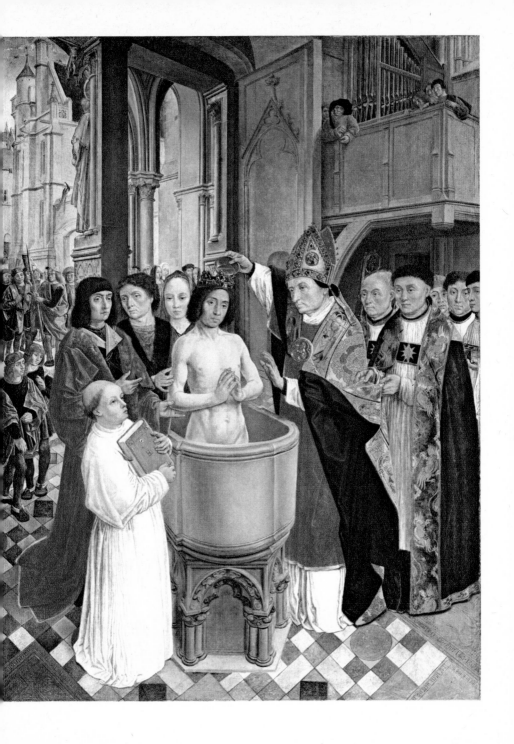

MASTER OF HEILIGENKREUZ (Franco-Austrian, early XV Century)
THE DEATH OF ST CLARE   Wood
Catalogue No. 1162   Height 26¹/₈" (66.4 cm.)
                                                       Width 21³/₈" (54.5 cm.)

St Clare, an ardent follower of St Francis of Assisi, founded the Second
Order of the Poor Clares, which flourished throughout Italy and appeared
also in Spain, France, and Germany, where this picture was painted. She
died in 1253 at Assisi.

In this scene of St Clare's death the Master of Heiligenkreuz conveys
a sense of the protective love of God. According to contemporary biographers, when St Clare died, Christ appeared above her bed and received
her soul; and the Virgin, followed by crowned and garlanded virgin martyrs, bent over her, and in her last moment supported her head. The
martyrs with Our Lady are: St Catherine of Alexandria, with her wheel;
St Cecilia, carrying a wreath of roses; St Barbara, with her tower; St
Dorothea, with a basket of flowers; and St Margaret, with a dragon.
St Agnes of Rome with her lamb stands in the foreground.

The elongated proportions of these figures with their long spidery fingers
give them a spectral appearance. This is stressed by their greater scale
compared to the nuns in the lower corner, who seem unaware of the
heavenly visitors. The burnished gold background, engraved with angels
carrying flags and musical instruments, heightens the unearthly effect and
suggests the splendor of celestial light.

The identity of the Master of Heiligenkreuz remains a mystery. He seems
to have been an itinerant master of the International Style. Very likely
he had some connection with Prague, one of the cosmopolitan art centers
in the second half of the fourteenth century. At the beginning of the fifteenth century, when the Hussite Wars broke out, many artists left Bohemia
and spread out in all directions. The Master of Heiligenkreuz may have
been one of these refugee artists. The picture reproduced formed the right
wing of a diptych; the other wing, representing the Death of the Virgin
Mary, is now in the Cleveland Museum of Art. Collections: Monastery in
northeast Germany; Professor Walter Schnakenberg; Dr Carl Langbehn,
Munich. *Samuel H. Kress Collection,* 1951. Painted c.1410.

MASTER OF THE ST BARTHOLOMEW ALTAR
(School of Cologne, active, c. 1470—c. 1510)

THE BAPTISM OF CHRIST

Catalogue No. 1630

Wood

Height 41³/₄″ (106.1 cm.)
Width 67¹/₈″ (170.5 cm.)

It is a charming fantasy and typically Northern to have the Christian martyrs and other saints see the Baptism of Our Lord. In eternity historical time does not exist. The fourteen saints are, from left to right: St Dorothea, with her basket of flowers; St Andrew, leaning on the X-shaped cross on which he was crucified; St Christopher, patron saint of travelers, carrying the Christ Child on his shoulders; St Jerome, wearing the red hat of a cardinal; St Catherine of Alexandria, carrying her wheel of martyrdom; St Augustine, holding a heart pierced by an arrow; and St Agnes, holding a lamb. At the other side of God the Father are: St Francis, showing the stigmata; St Lucy, who is slain by the sword; St Elizabeth of Thuringia, identified by her three crowns; St Anthony Abbot, with his staff; St Apollonia, patroness of dentists, holding a tooth in a pair of pincers; St Mary Magdalen, with her jar of precious ointment; and St George, in armor, with the vanguished dragon.

This is an unusual representation in Christian art, but it has a particular meaning. When fourteen saints are shown together in this way, they may usually be interpreted as the Holy Helpers, whose assistance could be invoked in dire emergencies. The Passion of Christ and the suffering of the martyrs are symbolized by the purple columbine growing on the river bank in the foreground.

The artist's name derives from the great altarpiece dedicated to St Bartholomew in the Church of St Columba in Cologne. He was evidently one of the best craftsmen of the time, for his work has lasted remarkably well. The rich coloring of the painting, the bizarre invention, and the careful execution of details explain why he has often been called the Northern Crivelli. Collections: According to tradition the painting was originally in a church in Arnheim; Count Baryas, Paris; Richard von Kaufmann, Berlin; O. Henkell, Wiesbaden. *Samuel H. Kress Collection*, 1955. Painted c. 1500.

MATHIS GRÜNEWALD (German, c. 1465–1528)
THE SMALL CRUCIFIXION   Wood
Catalogue No. 1379   Height 24¹/₄" (61.6 cm.)
                                         Width 18¹/₈" (46 cm.)

Heir to the Gothic and precursor of the Baroque, Grünewald has in this painting attained an intensity of expression no other artist has surpassed. The hands and feet of Christ stab at one's heart. Twisted and tortured, they are visual symbols of physical agony. His torso, 'dark smirched with pain,' is drawn in by a paroxysm of suffering. John and the two Marys show their anguish with gestures prayerful but helpless. The mood of ineffable woe is enhanced by the dark gloom of night, and by the colors: murky greens, livid blues, and blood reds.

The Small Crucifixion is one of scarcely more than a dozen paintings by Grünewald, and the only picture by him west of Colmar, the site of his great *Isenheim Altarpiece*. It was known to Sandrart who saw the panel in the possession of Duke Maximilian I of Bavaria. It had previously been owned, Sandrart tells us, by Maximilian's father, Duke William of Bavaria, an 'intelligent judge and connoisseur of fine art.' Sandrart writes of it as follows: '[Duke William] had a small Crucifixion with Our Dear Lady and St John, together with a kneeling and devoutly praying Mary Magdalen, most carefully painted by his [Grünewald's] hand, and he [the Duke] loved it very much, even without knowing whom it was by. On account of the wonderful Christ on the Cross, so suspended and supported on the feet, it is so very rare that real life could not surpass it and certainly it is more true to nature and reality than all Crucifixions when one contemplates it with thoughtful patience for a long time. For this reason it was, on the gracious order of the honorable Duke, engraved, half a sheet large, on copper in the year 1605 by Raphael Sadeler, and I pleased His Highness, the Great Elector Maximilian, of blessed memory, greatly since I made known the master's name.' It is a name that has fascinated art historians ever since. A list made twenty years ago of the most significant publications on Mathis Grünewald since 1914 listed 436 books and articles. He is the only painter whose life has served as the inspiration for a successful opera, *Mathis der Maler* by Hindemith. Collections: Duke William V of Bavaria; Duke Maximilian I of Bavaria; Landrat Dr Friedrich Schöne, Essen; Franz Wilhelm Koenigs and heirs, Haarlem. *Samuel H. Kress Collection*, 1953. Painted c. 1505–1510.

ALBRECHT DÜRER (German, 1471–1528)
MADONNA AND CHILD   Wood
Catalogue No. 1099   Height 19³/₄″ (50.2 cm.)
             Width 15⁵/₈″ (39.7 cm.)

In the year 1506 Albrecht Dürer wrote a famous letter to his friend Willibald Pirckheimer in which he said, 'But Sanbellinus [Giovanni Bellini] has praised me highly before several noblemen and he wishes to have something of my painting. He came himself and asked me to do something for him, saying that he would pay me well for it and all the people here tell me what a good man he is, so that I am greatly inclined to him. He is very old, but yet he is the best painter of them all.'

The written tribute paid to Giovanni Bellini by Dürer is well known. But a still greater compliment from the Northern painter to the Venetian master is the Madonna reproduced, which was once thought to be by Bellini himself, so close is it to the work of that artist. Here Dürer was searching, as have many other Germans, among the Italian painters for absolute beauty. But his creation remains as essentially Northern as the landscape glimpsed through the window, or the escutcheons at the lower corners, one of which has been identified as belonging to the Haller family who came from Dürer's home town, Nuremberg.

A number of critics have dated the painting in the last years of the fifteenth century, but more recently there has been a tendency to place it sometime after 1504 for a very good reason. The position of the Child's left arm, with the hand holding an apple, agrees almost precisely with the left arm and hand of Eve in Dürer's engraving of Adam and Eve dated 1504. Did Dürer intend this detail of the painting to refer to the Fall, repeating in the Child born to redeem Mankind the gesture of the Eve in his recently executed engraving?

On the back of the panel Lot and his daughters are shown fleeing from Sodom and Gomorrah (page 265). Collections: Colonel a'Court-Repington, London; Mrs. Phyllis Loder, London, Dr Heinrich Baron Thyssen-Bornemisza (Schloss Rohoncz), Villa Favorita, Lugano. *Samuel H. Kress Collection*, 1950. Painted probably between 1504 and 1507.

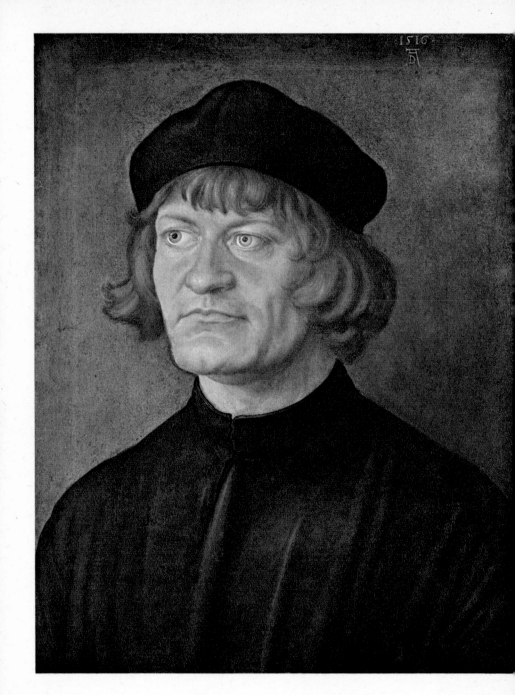

ALBRECHT DÜRER (German, 1471–1528)
PORTRAIT OF A CLERGYMAN   Parchment on Canvas
Catalogue No. 1100   Height 16⁷/₈″ (42.9 cm.)
                                           Width 13″ (33.2 cm.)

This famous portrait from the Czernin Collection, Vienna, is signed with
Dürer's monogram and dated 1516. Though the subject has not been identified, the portrait is a brilliant example of Dürer's ability to 'lay open the
fine net-work of the heart and brain of man,' to make us see deep into the
soul until we understand, for example, the character of this ugly, resolute
individual, whose personality, flashing out through luminous and asymmetrical eyes, exerts a powerful spell. His is the face of the Reformation.
Here one sees that burning fanaticism which, occurring on both sides,
caused the religious wars and, after a deluge of blood and destruction,
left Northern Europe bleak and desolate.

Dürer was not only capable of suggesting in his portraits the universal
in the individual, he was also able to give a remarkable record of physical
appearance. Trained by his work as an engraver and designer of woodcuts, he drew every form with the utmost precision. A trick of verisimili-
tude he often employed, until it became almost a signature, was to delineate
the windowpanes of his studio as though reflected in the pupils of his
sitter's eyes.

The technique of this painting is unusual. It is executed on parchment.
Artists were constantly seeking new methods and materials, and in 1516
Dürer tried twice the skin of a goat or sheep as a support for his painting.
Though the experiment apparently did not satisfy him, this portrait has
lasted without a blemish, and one wonders why he abandoned an inter-
esting innovation. Collections: Paul de Praun, Nuremberg; Count Jo-
hann Rudolf Czernin von Chudenitz, Vienna; Czernin Gallery, Vienna.
Samuel H. Kress Collection, 1950. Signed with monogram, and dated 1516.

PARVVLE PATRISSA, PATRIÆ VIRTVTIS ET HÆRES
ESTO, NIHIL MAIVS MAXIMVS ORBIS HABET.
GNATVM VIX POSSVNT COELVM ET NATVRA DEDISSE,
HVIVS QVEM PATRIS, VICTVS HONORET HONOS.
ÆQVATO TANTVM, TANTI TV FACTA PARENTIS,
VOTA HOMINVM, VIX QVO PROGREDIANTVR, HABENT
VINCITO, VICISTI, QVOT REGES PRISCVS ADORAT
ORBIS, NEC TE QVI VINCERE POSSIT, ERIT.

HANS HOLBEIN THE YOUNGER (German, 1497–1543)

EDWARD VI AS A CHILD   Wood
Catalogue No. 64   Height 22³/₈″ (57 cm.)
           Width 17³/₈″ (44 cm.)

This panel, painted soon after Holbein's second arrival in England, was given to Henry VIII on New Year's Day 1539. It is listed in the Royal Inventory as 'By Hanse Holbyne a table of the pictour of the p'nce [Prince's] grace.' The King was undoubtedly pleased with the likeness, for according to the same document, he gave 'To Hanse Holbyne, paynter, a gilte cruse [a type of cup] wt a cover Cornelis weing X oz. quarter.'

The poem at the bottom of the picture was written by Cardinal Morison, an influential figure of the Church and Court. It urges Edward to emulate his illustrious father in every way, presumably in matrimony as in other matters. Healthy as the young Prince seems in this portrait, fate did not give him time to marry even once, for he died at the age of fifteen.

The English were easily pleased in matters of art. Since the monkish illuminators of the Middle Ages they had never produced or imported a painter of the first rank. Therefore when Holbein arrived from Switzerland his popularity was enormous. He was particularly admired for his ability to ennoble his sitters. Here, commissioned to paint a portrait of a child not yet two years old, he manages to convey rank and majesty. The future monarch of England is dressed in courtly clothes of gold and velvet; he holds his rattle as though it were a scepter; and he raises his right hand in a gesture of royal magnanimity. Thus effigy becomes a symbol rather than a portrait. Holbein has presented the quintessence of royalty, the embodiment of the princely infant. Collections: English Royal Collection; Arundel (where engraved in 1650); Provincial Museum, Hannover (from the Royal and Ducal Hanoverian Collections). *Mellon Collection, 1937.* Painted presumably in 1538.

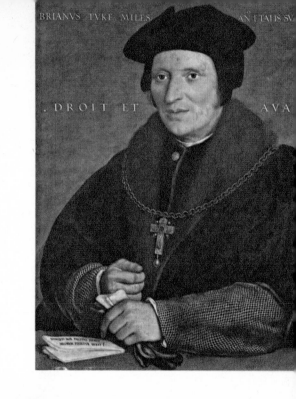

BRIANVS TVKE MILES AN TATIS SV

DROIT ET AVA

HANS HOLBEIN THE YOUNGER (German, 1497–1543)   Wood
SIR BRIAN TUKE
Catalogue No. 65   Height 19³/₈" (49 cm.)
                                                    Width 15¹/₄" (39 cm.)

As Hazlitt said, Holbein's portraits are like state documents. In them we
find recorded objectively, but with impressive dignity, the great figures who
surrounded Henry VIII. Sir Brian Tuke was governor of the King's post
'in England and in other parts of the King's domain beyond the sea.' He
was also secretary and treasurer of the royal household, and he has been
credited with the responsibility of bringing Holbein to England, possibly
to paint this portrait, which is the finest of a number of versions.

Droit et Avant (upright and forward) was the sitter's personal motto,
one that seems to have been justified by his life. On the folded paper near
his hand can be discerned with difficulty the Latin words from Job 10:20,
'Are not my days few? cease then, and let me alone, that I may take
comfort a little.' Sir Brian was fifty-seven when he was painted, an old

Continued on page 128

LUCAS CRANACH THE ELDER (German, 1472–1553)   Wood
A PRINCE OF SAXONY
Catalogue No. 896   Height 17¹/₈" (43.5 cm.)
                                                    Width 13¹/₂" (34.5 cm.)

Lucas Cranach painted the two famous portraits of a young prince and
princess tentatively identified by Friedländer and Rosenberg as the children
of Duke George the Bearded, of Saxony. One is reproduced opposite in
color, the other in black and white (page 266). The brother and sister, with
their long flaxen hair, their brocaded clothes and intricate jewelry, have
the unembarrassed serenity of children taught to face the ritual of social life.

It is interesting to contrast these portraits with Holbein's Edward VI
(page 116). Cranach's children are young nobles dressed up for a party;
whereas Holbein's prince is an infant monarch in his robes of state. Cranach
was a regional painter working in an unsophisticated principality; Holbein,
a cosmopolitan artist familiar with the great courts of Europe. But of the
two it is Cranach who, in his prosaic way, appeals to us. For it is he who
has penetrated to what we deem the reality of childhood, to what we adults
like to consider, rightly or wrongly, the wistfulness and guilelessness of
youth. Collections: A. Salomon, Dresden. *Ralph and Mary Booth Collection,* 1947. Painted c.1517.

119

HIERONYMUS BOSCH (Flemish, c. 1450—1516)   Wood
Death and the Miser   Height 36⅝″ (93 cm.)
Catalogue No. 1112   Width 12⅛″ (31 cm.)

The Dance of Death and the *Ars Moriendi* obsessed many European artists in the fifteenth and sixteenth centuries. However, death's conquest has never been treated more dramatically than in this wing from an altarpiece by Hieronymus Bosch, whose painting so strongly influenced Pieter Bruegel the Elder. On this long, narrow panel a sermon on avarice is enacted. In the foreground are weapons and pieces of armor, symbols of power, the original source of wealth. With age, wealth is first hoarded; then increased through usury; and in the end rats and salamanders become its agents. The rich man has, tied to his waist, his rosary and the key to his strongbox. These determine the final scene, the last transaction. Which will he choose? If he chooses the rosary he will look up, as his guardian angel pleads, yearning that he shall see the crucifix and be saved. If the key to his earthly treasures is also the key to his heart, the demon peering down from above the bed will be the victor. We can find the answer in the *Ars Moriendi*. According to its anonymous author the sleeper awakens, cries to God to protect him, and thereafter dedicates himself to religion. Thus the dying man gives back his gold to Mammon whose toad face appears under the curtain, and the

Continued on page 124

PIETER BRUEGEL THE ELDER (Flemish, c. 1525–1569)   Wood
The Temptation of St Anthony   Height 23″ (58.4 cm.)
Catalogue No. 1102   Width 33¾″ (85.7 cm.)

Psychoanalysis is a discovery of our time, but Pieter Bruegel the Elder, centuries ago, seems to have explored the unconscious. In this picture he has painted some personal nightmare, but it is a dream that might come to any of us. The strange warfare in the sky evokes a terror from above, while below we feel ourselves immobilized by horror, unable to escape into leafy bowers from the burning churches and the evil things that threaten us. Paintings like this are the product of an age of anxiety, an age of conflicting ideologies not unlike our own times. In Flanders in the sixteenth century there was on the one hand the anguish and fanaticism of reform and on the other the soldiers of the Duke of Alva trying in vain with blood and fire to reforge the lost unity of Europe. Collections: Countess Montblanc, Belgium. *Samuel H. Kress Collection,* 1950. Painted probably between 1555 and 1558.

RAPHAEL (Umbrian, 1483–1520)   Wood
ST GEORGE AND THE DRAGON   Height 11¹/₈″ (28.5 cm.)
Catalogue No. 26   Width 8³/₈″ (21.5 cm.)

Raphael was twenty-two or twenty-three when he painted *St George and the Dragon*. He had already become one of the most acomplished masters in Italy. No painting reveals more clearly his serenity, his effortless achievement. But there has been a reaction against the 'very rightness of Raphael's perfection.' Appreciation has shifted. The lofty pinnacles of art are today often considered boring, and critics prefer to study the arduous ascent to these heights, to trace the tortuous route leading from the incompetent to the proficient. Thus the romantic basis of contemporary aesthetics has blinded many people to the beauty of Raphael's paintings.

This point of view, the exaltation of the half-realized, the half-expressed, accords with the art of our time. Modern painters lack the very qualities for which Raphael was pre-eminent. For more than a century painters have brought to their craft less and less of that easy fluency of draftsmanship, that simple felicity of composition which Raphael took for granted. We have come to despise facility largely because facility of a high order has almost ceased to exist. Drawn by instinctive sympathy to contemporary art, many people, especially painters, have come to look on Raphael's work with prejudice. But his great paintings, such as the picture reproduced, should not be judged by the standards prevalent today. They should be judged by the standards which Sir Joshua Reynolds termed 'the great style,' and which in Italy is termed the *gusto grande,* and in France the *beau idéal.* For these are the terms of excellence which people of culture have accepted for over four hundred years. If we use them as a measure of Raphael's achievement, we shall find that he has given us a supreme expression of the classical style. Collections: Commissioned by Duke Guidobaldo da Montefeltro, the ruler of Urbino, and taken as a gift to Henry VII of England by Count Baldassare Castiglione; Third Earl of Pembroke (engraved by L. Vorsterman in 1627); Fourth Earl of Pembroke gave it to Charles I of England in exchange for the Holbein drawings now at Windsor Castle (reproduced in tapestry at the royal factory at Mortlake); Henry Hurault, Comte de Cheverny; Marquise d'Aumont; Abbé de La Noüe; Lauret Le Tessier de Montarsy; Charles d'Escoubleau; Marquis de Sourdis; Pierre Crozat; Louis-François Crozat, Marquis de Châtel; Louis-Antoine Crozat, Baron de Thiers; Catherine II, Empress of Russia; Hermitage Gallery, Leningrad. *Mellon Collection,* 1937. Signed. Painted 1504/05.

RAPHAEL (Umbrian, 1483–1520) Wood
THE SMALL COWPER MADONNA Height 23⁷/₁₆″ (59.5 cm.)
Catalogue No. 653 Width 17³/₈″ (44 cm.)

The Small Cowper Madonna was purchased in Italy in the eighteenth century by that remarkable Earl Cowper who is referred to frequently in Horace Walpole's correspondence with Sir Horace Mann, and was hung for over a century in his country estate of Panshanger. A great connoisseur with an instinctive sympathy for the Renaissance, Lord Cowper was so drawn to Italy that he spent most of his life in Florence and became a prince of the Holy Roman Empire.

But though Walpole might despise Lord Cowper's choice of titles, he could not but envy his choice of pictures. For this eccentric English Earl was the only collector of his time who could show the span of Raphael's development during his Florentine period. The two Madonnas, which were in his collection and which are now both in the National Gallery of Art (page 266) reveal the quintessence of Raphael's early and best manner of painting on panel. Giovanni Morelli, the founder of the system on which the modern attribution of Italian painting is based, considered *The Small Cowper Madonna* to be 'perhaps the most lovely of all Raphael's Madonnas ... [it] sets the young artist before our eyes in the full blaze of his independence.' In the half-century that has elapsed since Morelli made this statement, no serious critic has questioned either his evaluation or his placing of the picture in Raphael's development. There has been general agreement among critics that *The Small Cowper Madonna* was probably painted sometime in the year 1505, shortly after Raphael achieved his mature style in Florence. Our Lady's expression still retains the dry, tired wistfulness we find in the Madonnas and saints painted by his master, Perugino, but the figures are drawn with more certainty, their forms modeled with more solidity than in any work of the Umbrian period. Collections: *Widener Collection*, 1942. Painted probably 1505.

Continued from page 120
drama has a happy ending. But we have overlooked one character in the scene. Leaning on the threshold is a winged manikin. He appears so often in paintings by Bosch that he is almost a signature. Is this perhaps a portrait of the artist himself who, with a twisted, sardonic smile, meditates sceptically on his own sermon? Collections: Baron Joseph van der Elst, Bruges. *Samuel H. Kress Collection*, 1951. Probably painted c. 1490, as the outside of the left wing of an altarpiece.

124

RAPHAEL (Umbrian, 1483–1520)

THE ALBA MADONNA　　　　　　Transferred from wood to canvas

Catalogue No. 24　　　　　　　Diameter 37¹/₄″ (94.5 cm.)

The Alba Madonna was painted about 1509, just after Raphael had arrived in Rome and fallen under the spell of Michelangelo. It is one of the supreme compositional achievements of Renaissance painting, for balance in a tondo, or round picture, required the utmost delicacy in adjustment. If the masses are not in equilibrium, the picture will seem to roll like a wheel. In the *Alba Madonna* this complex problem is solved and the result is one of extraordinary stability.

The picture was taken to Spain at the end of the seventeenth century and remained in the collection of the Dukes of Alba for more than a hundred years. It was eventually sold by that family on orders of the King, Carlos IV, to the Queen's lover, Manuel Godoy; and on his disgrace and arrest in 1808 it was auctioned. The prices paid for the picture in the last century are an interesting gauge of the rise in value of works of art. About 1820 *The Alba Madonna* was sold in London for £4,000 ($20,000); in 1836 it was bought by Czar Nicholas I for the Hermitage, Leningrad, for £14,000 ($70,000); and in 1931 it was acquired by Mr. Mellon for $1,166,400. Thus its monetary value increased roughly fourteen times in 95 years and fifty times in 111 years.

But one must bear in mind that the purchasing power of money has also decreased. Recently a Rembrandt, *Aristotle with a Bust of Homer*, was sold in New York for $2,300,000. According to the Bureau of Labor Statistics, between 1932 and 1961 the buying power of the dollar diminished by more than 50 per cent, so that thirty years later $2,300,000 is slightly less than the equivalent in purchasing power of $1,166,400. This devaluation of currency explains to some extent the constant rise of prices being paid for works of art, even for modern art, where scarcity can hardly be said to exist. Collections: Church of Monte Oliveto, Nocera de' Pagani near Naples; Don Gaspar Méndez de Haro y Guzmán, Naples; Dukes of Alba, Madrid; Don Manuel Godoy, Principe de la Paz; Count Edmond de Bourke, Danish Ambassador to Spain; W. G. Coesvelt, London; Czar Nicholas I for the Hermitage Gallery, Leningrad. *Mellon Collection*, 1937. Painted c. 1509.

FLORENTINE SCHOOL, XVI Century   Wood
ALLEGORICAL PORTRAIT OF DANTE   Height 50" (126.9 cm.)
Catalogue No. 1609   Width 47¹/₄" (120 cm.)

This portrait of Dante is a remarkable discovery made quite recently in
an English collection. Its attribution remains a mystery. Pontormo has been
suggested; Bacchiacca is another candidate. But neither ascription is
entirely satisfactory. There can, however, be no doubt that whoever
painted this canvas has given us the noblest ideal portrait of Dante which
has survived from the Renaissance.

The poet sits brooding over the mystery of the temporary and the
eternal, the city of man and the city of God. Below his protective hand is
Florence fitfully illumined by the fires of Hell. Across the Stygian river
he gazes at the Monte Sancto di Dio silhouetted against the ineffable light
of Paradise. His left hand holds a manuscript codex of the *Paradiso* open
to a page of *Canto* XXV, 'Se mai continga...' (If it should ever hap-
pen...), the famous passage which expresses his wistful hope that one day
he might be welcomed back from exile and crowned poet laureate in the
Baptistry opposite the Cathedral which was for so long the center of his
life. This moving tribute to the most famous of all Florentines was painted
two centuries after his death.

Collections: Graham, London; Lord Hailsham, London. *Samuel H. Kress
Collection*, 1956. Painted c. 1530.

Continued from page 119

man by the standards of his time. He accepted that he had but a short
while to live, for in the Renaissance death was always imminent. The
plague still ravaged Europe, and an outbreak of the pestilence in London
some years later carried off Holbein himself when only forty-six and at
the peak of his career. If a courtier escaped death by disease there was still
the enmity of his monarch to be feared; and this could be mortal too, as it
was in the case of St Thomas More, the friend both of Tuke and Holbein,
who died with many others for refusing to say 'yes' to the King. Sir Brian
never lost his sovereign's favor; but in his twisted smile, full of pain, and
in the wistful plea on the folded paper, we sense the desperate insecurity
of life in the England of Henry VIII. Collections: Philip Sidney, Third
Earl of Leicester; Sir Paul Methuen, and descendants, Corsham Court,
Wiltshire; Richard Sanderson, Edinburgh; Richard, Second Marquess of
Westminster; *Mellon Collection*, 1937. Painted 1526–28.

LORENZO LOTTO (Venetian, c. 1480–1556)
ALLEGORY   Wood
Catalogue No. 267   Height 22¼" (56 cm.)
                                          Width 17⅛" (43 cm.)

In July 1505, Lorenzo Lotto completed a portrait of Bernardo Rossi, who was Bishop of Treviso from 1499 to 1527. This painting is now one of the masterpieces of the Naples Museum. Some years ago the picture reproduced was discovered, and on the back of the panel was an inscription identifying it as the cover for Rossi's portrait. Such covers were often hinged, thus forming with the portrait itself a diptych. Their purpose remains obscure: perhaps the sitter wished his likeness to be seen only by intimate friends; perhaps he wished to protect the portrait itself; or perhaps he welcomed the opportunity that this additional panel offered for a further symbolic interpretation of his character or his life. This latter allegorical intention seems to have motivated Bernardo Rossi. That he was interested in allegory is indicated by his portrait medal, which is also in the National Gallery of Art. This has on the reverse a female figure in tunic and mantle, holding a sunflower and standing in a car drawn by an eagle and a winged dragon.

The meaning of Lotto's *Allegory* is less baffling than its medallic counterpart. The painted cover seems to present in figurative terms the desirability of choosing virtue instead of vice. On the left, a naked child bathed in sunlight is picking up instruments: a compass, a square, a flute, a scroll, symbols of cultural pursuits and thus for the Renaissance man symbols of the virtuous life. The right side of the picture is devoted to an allegory of vice. The light has gone, and in the umbraceous gloom a drunken satyr sprawls among overturned vessels, while in the distance a ship founders in the storm. Lotto tactfully indicates that his sitter has triumphed over passion and won his way to virtue. Rossi's winged spirit is shown climbing rapidly upward on a steep and stony path toward the summit of a mountain where the sky is clearing. Collections: Probably Garden Palace of the Farnese, Parma (XVII century); Antonio Bertoli, Parma; Giacomo Gritti, Bergamo. *Samuel H. Kress Collection*, 1935. Painted 1505.

DOSSO DOSSI (Ferrarese, c. 1479–c. 1542)   Canvas
CIRCE AND HER LOVERS IN A LANDSCAPE   Height 39⁵/₈″ (100 cm.)
Catalogue No. 716   Width 53¹/₂″ (136 cm.)

There are paintings which, like 'huge cloudy symbols of a high romance,' never cease to challenge the imagination, to promise the revelation of some hidden secret. In the canvas by Dosso Dossi a nude woman, seated in an idyllic landscape, is surrounded by birds and beasts. Who is she and why does she point, like one of Michelangelo's sibyls, toward an inscribed tablet? The scene fits the legend of Circe, who turned men into animals; but absent are those wolves, lions, and swine Ulysses saw when he encountered 'that awful Goddess of the luxuriant tresses, own sister to the wizard Aeëtes.' A transformation in the story has taken place. The animals are now the most charming and gentle of beasts, and even the lioness is more heraldic than savage.   *Continued on page 137*

GIORGIONE (Venetian, c. 1478–1510)   Wood
THE ADORATION OF THE SHEPHERDS   Height 35³/₄″ (91 cm.)
Catalogue No. 400   Width 53¹/₂″ (136 cm.)

What we have come to call the Giorgionesque was as revolutionary in the Renaissance as was Cubism in recent years. In the early Renaissance, paintings were thought of as colored drawings modeled in light and shade to suggest relief. Later artists observed that we do not normally see the separate contours of objects but that their forms seem to melt into each other and to fuse with the surrounding atmosphere. The crystalline clarity of early morning, which is characteristic of the fifteenth century and can be seen in the Botticelli *Adoration* (page 83), changes in the new style to the misty sunlight of late afternoon. This soft illumination increases unity of effect. Giorgione, who died in 1510, presumably at the age of thirty-two, has been credited with these innovations, which found their fullest development among Venetian painters. But actually the Giorgionesque, like Cubism, was a way of painting adopted simultaneously by a number of artists. *The Adoration of the Shepherds,* for example, has been attributed in turn to the three leading painters of Venice at the beginning of the six-teenth century, Giorgione, Bellini, and Titian.   *Continued on page 140*

GIOVANNI BELLINI (Venetian, c. 1430–1516)
THE FEAST OF THE GODS   Canvas
Catalogue No. 597   Height 67" (170 cm.)
                                                        Width 74" (188 cm.)

The connoisseurship of painting offers, from time to time, investigations as fascinating and complex as a detective story. *The Feast of the Gods,* for example, is signed Giovanni Bellini. Yet Titian, according to Vasari, brought it to completion. A composite X-ray of the painting made recently indicates that the picture has had three backgrounds. There is evidence that the final alterations, and perhaps the earlier changes as well, are due to Titian. As far as one can tell, his motives were mixed; but the impelling reason seems to be have been that the original design did not harmonize with the other pictures in the same room in the Castle of Ferrara which Alfonso d'Este asked him to paint: *Bacchus and Ariadne,* now in London, and *The Venus Worship* and *The Andrians,* now in Madrid.

Though Titian finally transformed the background of *The Feast of the Gods* into a landscape which has been judged 'the finest that up to that time had ever been painted ... an epoch in the history of art,' still, from the beginning, Bellini's painting was an astounding innovation. One remarkable feature is the representation of the gods and goddesses in the guise of everyday people. It is as though they had become players in a Renaissance masque. The scene they act out, a story told by Ovid, explains the annual sacrifice made by the Romans to Priapus. On the left the ass of Silenus brays and arouses the drowsy deities as, on the right, the god of fertility secretly approaches the goddess of chastity. Then, as Ovid says, 'The nymph in terror started up ... and flying gave the alarm to the whole grove; ... the god in the moonlight was laughed at by all.' However, at the touch of Bellini's brush the ribald joke undergoes a metamorphosis, becomes a noble Dionysiac mystery, much as Shakespeare's alchemy transmutes leaden stories into golden plays. Collections: Duke Alfonso I d'Este, Ferrara; Cardinal Pietro Aldobrandini and family, Rome; Vincenzo Camuccini, Rome; Duke of Northumberland, Alnwick Castle, England. *Widener Collection,* 1942. Signed, and dated 1514.

TITIAN (Venetian, c. 1477–1576)　　　　　　　　　　　Canvas
Doge Andrea Gritti　　　　　　　　　　　Height 51¹/₂″ (130.8 cm.)
Catalogue No. 1408　　　　　　　　　　　Width 41¹/₂″ (105.4 cm.)

The seal of Charles I of England and a label reading, 'Bought for his Majesty in Italy in 1626,' are still preserved on the back of the canvas of this stupendous portrait, more recently in the Czernin Collection in Vienna. The royal catalogue also listed it: 'Duke Grettie, of Venice, with his right hand holding his robes. Bought by the King, half figures so big as the life, in a black wooden gilded frame.' Perhaps Charles saw in the stern, implacable face of the Venetian Doge those traits of character he himself lacked. Titian has dowered Gritti with a grim, ruthless personality and made him a symbol of the power of the galleys that, under the patronage of St Mark, caused Venice to be honored and feared along the trade routes of the world. But Gritti was also a patron of the arts. At his order, a considerable number of Titian's large religious, historical, and allegorical pictures, now mostly lost, were painted.

The hand with which the Doge grasps his flowing cape may be based upon the hand of Moses in the famous statue by Michelangelo in Rome. A Venetian sculptor, Jacopo Sansovino, is believed to have brought a cast of this hand to Venice, where Titian probably studied its massive power to help him create an image of uncompromising majesty, the archetype of an imperious ruler. Collections: King Charles I of England; Wenzel Anton, Prince von Kaunitz-Rietburg, Chancellor of Empress Maria Theresa; Count Johann Rudolf Czernin von Chudenitz, Vienna; Czernin Gallery, Vienna. *Samuel H. Kress Collection*, 1954. Signed. Painted probably between 1535 and 1540.

Continued from page 133
There is a clue to this change. In the court of Ferrara, where this picture was probably painted, Ariosto had composed his famous *Orlando Furioso*, setting forth a new version of the Circean myth. In his romantic epic Alcina is the perfect example of the beautiful and seductive woman. Like Circe she changes her lovers into animals; but instead of doing this with the touch of a wand, as Homer describes the transformation of the followers of Ulysses, she uses esoteric incantations. These in Dosso Dossi's canvas are symbolized by the tablet and the cabalistic book with which Alcina – for the nude figure is probably she – holds her court of wild creatures spellbound. Collections: William Graham; Robert H. and Evelyn Benson, London. *Samuel H. Kress Collection*, 1942. Painted c. 1514/16.

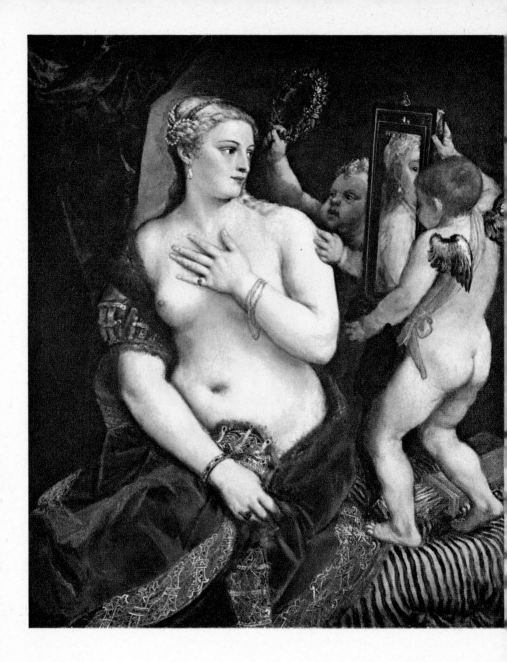

TITIAN (Venetian, c. 1477–1576)
VENUS WITH A MIRROR   Canvas
Catalogue No. 34   Height 49" (124.5 cm.)
                                               Width 41½" (105.5 cm.)

Titian, more than any other Renaissance artist, understood the spirit of
classical art. Yet he was nearly seventy when he went to Rome and had
his first opportunity to visit the capital of the ancient world and to see
the great works of art accumulated there. When he was not executing his
many important missions at the Vatican and among the Roman nobility
he was, 'learning from the marvelous, ancient stones,' as he said. Though
he regretted that he had not received this inspiration earlier, still it came
at a time when he was about to enter upon his period of supreme achievement, which lasted until he was well into his nineties. Under the influence
of classical art his late nudes gained an amplitude of form, a heavy
magnificence which suggests Greek sculpture of the Golden Age.

From his earliest masterpieces like the Bacchanals, painted for the Duke
of Ferrara, to canvases like this, painted when he was over seventy, Titian
repeatedly celebrated the goddess of love. All these pictures are permeated
with a sensuality which deepens with age, growing always more impersonal. In his final work he expresses the indwelling power of feminine
beauty, a quality which transcends the loveliness of any individual woman.
These pictures are his final homage to Venus, as moving in their way as
the late love poems of Yeats.

Titian painted several variations on the theme of Venus with a mirror,
and still others were produced by followers and imitators, but this particular canvas he kept for himself, feeling for it perhaps some special
affection. After his death it was sold to the Barbarigo family by his son,
Pomponio. It remained in their possession until it was purchased by Nicholas I for the Hermitage Gallery, Leningrad. Collections: Pomponio Vecel-
lio, Venice; Barbarigo family, Venice; Hermitage Gallery, Leningrad.
Mellon Collection, 1937. Painted c. 1555.

TITIAN (Venetian, c. 1477–1576) Canvas
VENUS AND ADONIS Height 42" (122 cm.)
Catalogue No. 680 Width 53⅜" (135.5 cm.)

At a still later period, when he was over eighty, Titian painted this canvas showing Adonis tearing himself from the embrace of Venus to undertake his fatal hunt. These two figures from Greek mythology symbolize a recurring conflict in the human soul, the suffering that comes from unsatisfied passion, an emotion deeply rooted in human experience. Portents of the cruel death awaiting Adonis are disclosed in the stormy light bursting in the sky, the gesture of Venus clutching her lover with terror, and the attitude of Cupid huddled over his dove like an embodiment of his mother's fear.

The figures seem to transcend human form, to have become heroic shapes only vaguely related to physical reality. This gives to Titian's late works an unearthly quality, a preternatural appenarance. Titian's *Venus and Adonis* is a climax of the imaginative, pictorial mode of painting which begins with such pictures as *The Adoration of the Shepherds* by Giorgione (page 132).

Of the many versions of the composition, the present painting is considered the last executed by Titian himself. Collections: Lord Bristol (XVII century) and his descendants, among whom the last owner was the Seventh Earl Spencer. *Widener Collection,* 1942. Painted after 1560.

Continued from page 133

An increasing number of experts, however, believe the picture to be by Giorgione, and this is the attribution which most clearly describes its style. Bernard Berenson, the most famous of all critics of Italian art, remained adamant for many years in his opposition to ascribing this painting to Giorgione. Joseph Duveen, the art dealer who owned the picture at the time, tried in every way to make Berenson alter his opinion. This led to their celebrated quarrel. At the end of his life, however, Berenson did change his mind and concluded that the painting was at least in part by Giorgione, working in collaboration with Titian. Collections: Cardinal Fesch, Rome; Claudius Tarral, Paris; Thomas Wentworth Beaumont, Bretton Hall, Yorkshire; Lord Allendale, London. *Samuel H. Kress Collection,* 1938. Painted c. 1510.

MORETTO DA BRESCIA (Brescian, c. 1498–1554) Wood
PIETÀ Height 69¹/₈″ (175.8 cm.)
Catalogue No. 1093 Width 38³/₄″ (98.5 cm.)

By the late 1520s, when this painting was executed, leadership in Italian
art had passed to Venice, the capital of a republic which extended from
the head of the Adriatic to Lake Como. In expanding over this wide
territory a number of city-states were overrun, each of which had once
developed its own school of painting. Though the artists of these North
Italian schools recognized the suzerainty of the great Venetian masters,
their styles remained local and idiomatic. Thus the paintings of Moretto,
who was active in Brescia, a hill town on the western fringe of the Venetian Republic, are marked by a religious feeling hard to find in Venice
itself after Giovanni Bellini's death.

This *Pietà* is one of the most moving representations of this subject in
art. Here is a work of great sanctity and devotion, an expression of highest
tragedy. Collections: Earl of Egremont; Cook, Doughty House, Richmond,
Surrey. *Samuel H. Kress Collection*, 1947. Painted in the 1520s.

SODOMA (Sienese, 1477–1549) Wood
ST GEORGE AND THE DRAGON Height 55¹/₂″ (137.8 cm.)
Catalogue No. 1155 Width 38³/₈″ (97.6 cm.)

Though the majority of the great achievements in art are in the realm of
high tragedy, still there is enchantment to be found in certain paintings
that come close to comedy. Sodoma's *St George and the Dragon* is in this
lighter vein. The hero's horse is much fiercer than the poor contorted
monster he seems about to bite; and it is evident that St George, with his
broken barber's-pole spear, may plunge at any moment over the head of
his mount. The heroine rolls her eyes to heaven, and deliciously overacts
her part!

When the picture was acquired from the famous Cook Collection the
foreground was a flowering meadow. X-rays disclosed that some squeamish
collector had completely buried under repaint the remains of the dragon's
previous meal, eaten apparently just before the arrival of St George. The
meadow was cleaned away, and the picture now appears as originally
painted, with just that touch of gruesomeness so characteristic of fairy
tales. Collections: Seventeenth Earl of Shrewsbury, Alton Towers, Straf-
fordshire; Cook, Doughty House, Richmond, Surrey. *Samuel H. Kress
Collection*, 1947. Painted probably 1518.

142

GIOVANNI BATTISTA MORONI (Brescian, c. 1520–1578)
A GENTLEMAN IN ADORATION BEFORE THE MADONNA   Canvas
Catalogue No. 225   Height 23¹/₂″ (60 cm.)
                                                     Width 25¹/₂″ (65 cm.)

Little is known of Moroni's life except that he was active in the provincial town of Bergamo. His portraits, in which he revealed his true ability, his sensitive understanding of character, recall the work of his master Moretto who was active in nearby Brescia. The mood he creates is the same wistful melancholy that we find in Moretto's style. The figures in Moroni's portraits seem to implore our sympathy with a shy, solemn insistence. This elusive note of diffident sadness, so often to be found in provincial portraiture, is the opposite of the mood created by Titian, Veronese, and Tintoretto, in whose portraits we have a feeling of inner strength, a sense that the men and women they portray were destined by some ineluctable right to dominate, to possess the world.

Probably Moroni's provincial patrons lacked the self-assurance which is so conspicuous in the people who sat for the Venetian masters. Or perhaps this lack was in the artist himself, for Moroni never mastered the *gusto grande,* the grand manner, which was fashionable in his day. He never learned that art of ennobling, or amplifying the personalities of his sitters. He painted his subjects as he saw them; he delineated with touching fidelity the commoners and the petty nobility of a provincial town, men and women who were close to their peasants, who often helped in the vineyards and fields, and were not above undertaking menial tasks. His canvases mirror, perhaps better than the work of any other artist, the personalities of a small town in the sixteenth century.

In the painting of *A Gentleman in Adoration before the Madonna* Moroni was confronted with a subject common enough in Venetian art, a miraculous apparition. Titian, for instance, has often created such scenes with his easy invention, his great imaginative power; but Moroni, devoid of all visionary feeling, was paralyzed, as Berenson has said, the moment he was separated from the model. Thus in portraying the Madonna and Child he dared not trust his own creative genius. He turned instead to an engraving by Albrecht Dürer for his model. Yet the amazing fact remains that his painting triumphs over such naive imitation. Moroni's sensitive and poetic treatment of the kneeling man gives his picture a mood of intimate devotion, an atmosphere of fervent piety, which seems an echo from a simpler, more innocent world. Collections: Casa Grimani, Venice. *Samuel H. Kress Collection,* 1932. Painted c. 1560.

144

JACOPO TINTORETTO (Venetian, 1518–1594) Canvas
CHRIST AT THE SEA OF GALILEE
Catalogue No. 825 Height 46″ (117 cm.) Width 66¼″ (168.5 cm.)

Ask a contemporary painter to name the greatest of the Venetian artists and the chances are he will choose Tintoretto. There are many reasons for this choice, but in the painting reproduced one is especially evident: Tintoretto's emotional intensity. In *Christ at the Sea of Galilee*, the event illustrated is described in John 21. Our Lord, standing on the shore, reveals himself to his disciples who are fishing: 'Now when Simon Peter heard that it was the Lord, he girt his fisher's coat unto him, (for he was naked,) and did cast himself into the sea.' Here almost for the first time nature becomes an actor in the drama.

It is interesting to note that Hans Tietze, one of the most astute authorities on Venetian painting, always believed this picture to be by El Greco. The elongation of Christ, the color and modeling of the waves, and the emotional intensity of the scene suggest the Spanish painter. But it is hard to place the picture in the chronology of El Greco's works, and the touch in the smaller figures and the painting of the sky seem typical of Tintoretto's style. Collections: Count J. Galotti; Arthur Sachs, New York. *Samuel H. Kress Collection*, 1943. Painted c.1560.

EL GRECO (Spanish, 1541–1614) Wood
CHRIST CLEANSING THE TEMPLE Height 25¾″ (65.4 cm.)
Catalogue No. 1482 Width 32¾″ (83.2 cm.)

Christ Cleansing the Temple, by El Greco, an early work, perhaps the first he ever signed, reflects the influence of Titian, Tintoretto, and Veronese. It was painted when the young Greek had barely arrived in Venice, and on this canvas he signs his real name, *Domenikos Theotokópoulos*.

Many borrowings from Venetian painting are evident. The pose of the half-nude woman, lying on the ground with her arm behind her head, was copied from the sleeping Ariadne in Titian's early *Bacchanal;* the vigorous diagonal thrusts of the composition show Tintoretto's influence; while the voluptuous female types suggest Paolo Veronese's works. There is also a debt to the greatest master of Roman painting, Michelangelo, in the half-nude figure, seen from the back, at the left of Christ, which is based on two figures in Michelangelo's *Conversion of St Paul* in the Pauline Chapel in the Vatican. Collections: J. C. Robinson, London; Cook, Doughty House, Richmond, Surrey. *Samuel H. Kress Collection*, 1955. Signed. Painted c. 1570.

147

EL GRECO (Spanish, 1541–1614)
THE VIRGIN WITH ST INÉS AND ST TECLA   Canvas
Catalogue No. 622   Height 76¹/₈″ (193.5 cm.)
                                                Width 40¹/₂″ (103 cm.)

Among the Old Masters, the true prophet of modern art is El Greco. His
work foreshadows the abandonment three hundred years later of naturalism
for Expressionism, of proportions determined by nature for proportions
determined by emotion. Academic critics fighting this trend used to assert
that El Greco distorted the human form because his eyesight was defective.
We now believe that astigmatism affected him less, if at all, than the
stylization in Byzantine icons and mosaics he had seen as a young man on
his native island of Crete. But the fashion initiated by Parmigianino, that
vogue for tall, slender figures with small heads, which became modish in
European painting of the late sixteenth century, also played its part and
prepared the public to accept the exaggerated elongations El Greco found
suitable for his highly emotional style.

El Greco, however, was not merely a precursor of many contemporary
artists; he also expressed, through the flamelike forms he created, the spirit
of his own time, that ardent and mystical piety which followed the newly-
launched Counter Reformation. *The Virgin with St Inés and St Tecla,* once
in the chapel of San José in Toledo, the Spanish town which became El
Greco's final home, is a summit of such visionary painting. What more
marvelous rendering of substance at once tangible and intangible, corporeal
and incorporeal, than the cherubim who surround the Virgin? They seem
modeled in ectoplasm, formed of some emanation of thought. Even the
artist's signature, the initials of his Greek name (Domenikos Theotokópoulos)
traced on the forehead of St Tecla's lion, seems to have taken on symbolic
significance. The whole scene illustrates, so far as this is possible, the ex-
periences described by Greco's contemporary, St John of the Cross, and
other mystics.

But if El Greco himself was a mystic, he was a very practical one. We
know that he was an efficient painter, ran a profitable shop, and was ready
to repeat his pictures as many times as the market required. Even his
distortions did not diminish his popularity, for his paintings apparently
gave concrete and convincing form to visions that many pious people in
Spain had seen or hoped to see. Collections: Chapel of San José, Toledo
(until 1906). *Widener Collection,* 1942. Signed with initials. Painted 1597–99.

EL GRECO (Spanish, 1541–1614)
LAOCOÖN   Canvas
Catalogue No. 885   Height 54¹/₈″ (137.5 cm.)
                                          Width 67⁷/₈″ (172.5 cm.)

Although El Greco was Greek by birth, he ignored the mythology and
history of his fatherland. The only exception is this canvas of Laocoön and
his sons. Greco probably painted the picture for his own pleasure, a challenge to the famous sculpture group discovered in 1506, which was one of
the sights of Rome when he visited that city in 1570. A *Laocoön* was
listed in the inventory of his estate in 1614, and he may actually have been
working on this painting at the time of his death, for a recent cleaning
indicates that the three figures on the right of the picture remained unfinished.

The story of Laocoön, which El Greco illustrated with the most dramatic
and powerful composition he ever achieved, is told by Arctinus of Miletus
and repeated with some variations by Vergil. Laocoön was a priest of
Poseidon who warned his fellow Trojans not to carry into their city the
wooden horse left behind by the invading Greeks. But his famous words,
'Fools, trust not the Greeks, even when bearing gifts,' went unheeded. In
despair he hurled his spear against the horse, a gesture of sacrilege against
Minerva, to whom the wooden statue had been dedicated. The three deities
portrayed on the right of the canvas avenged this desecration by causing
sea-serpents to kill Laocoön and his two sons. Their deaths were interpreted by the Trojans as a sign of the anger of the gods, and the horse was
brought inside the city walls. At night Greek soldiers concealed inside its
belly crept out and opened the city gates, thus bringing about the fall of
Troy and ending the Trojan War. In the middle distance the wooden horse
can be seen, and in place of Troy is a view of Toledo, El Greco's adopted
home. Collections: Probably the large painting of Laocoön listed in 1614
in the inventory of El Greco's estate in Toledo; Dukes of Montpensier,
Seville; Palace of San Telmo, Seville; Infante Don Antonio de Orléans,
Sanlúcar de Barrameda; E. Fischer, Charlottenburg; Prince Paul of Yugo-
slavia, Belgrade. *Samuel H. Kress Collection,* 1945. Painted c.1610.

VELÁZQUEZ (Spanish, 1599–1660)   Canvas
POPE INNOCENT X   Height 19¹/₂″ (49 cm.) Width 16¹/₄″ (42 cm.)
Catalogue No. 80

When Thomas Moore visited the Palazzo Doria in Rome in 1819, he noted in his diary, 'It is here the famous portrait by Velásquez is (of Pope Pamfili) which Sir J.[oshua] Reynolds pronounced the finest picture in Rome. This and the St Michael of Guido were, they say, the only ones he condescended to copy.' The painting reproduced, a preliminary study for the Doria portrait, has an immediacy, a probing realism that goes even beyond the painting that aroused Reynolds' enthusiasm.

Both pictures were painted during Velázquez' second Italian journey (1649–1651) and may in fact have been an undisclosed reason for his visit to Italy. For Innocent X had changed the policy of the papacy. Whereas his predecessor, Urban VIII, had been sympathetic toward Mazarin and the French, Innocent shifted to the side of the Hapsburgs and Spain. It was only natural that the leading Spanish painter should be sent to do the portrait of so important an advocate of his country. But diplomacy did not affect Velázquez' integrity as an artist. He portrayed the Pope with absolute detachment. Collections: Walpole, Norfolk, England; Hermitage Gallery, Leningrad. *Mellon Collection*, 1937. Painted 1649–50.

VELÁZQUEZ (Spanish, 1599–1660)   Canvas
THE NEEDLEWOMAN   Height 29¹/₈″ (74 cm.) Width 23⁵/₈″ (60 cm.)
Catalogue No. 81

It would seem at first as though this study of a woman sewing were never finished. The left hand is merely blocked in, and the fingers of the right, barely indicated. But this device of adumbrating rather than defining shapes was used by Velázquez in a number of late works to suggest motion. The outlines of the fingers of Innocent X in the Doria picture (page 166) are blurred, an indistinction which makes them seem to twitch with nervous energy. Again there is the hand of the boy with his foot on the dog in *Las Meninas*, where a flickering movement is given by making the contours seem faltering or indiscernible; and in *Las Hilanderas* if one looks at the hand of the woman in the foreground, one sees what appears to be successive positions of her fingers as she winds her yarn. In all these pictures the vibrating effect of shifting planes of light conveys a sense of motion in a way that is new in art. Collections: Amédée, Marquis de Govello de Keriaval, Château de Kerlevenant, Sarzeau, Morbihan; Mme Christiane de Polés, Paris. *Mellon Collection*, 1937. Painted c. 1640.

BARTOLOMÉ ESTEBAN MURILLO (Spanish, 1617–1682)

A GIRL AND HER DUENNA   Canvas

Catalogue No. 642   Height 49³/₈″ (125.5 cm.)

                                      Width 41″ (105.5 cm.)

All the paintings we have reproduced so far have been either devotional pictures, mythological scenes, or portraits. In the seventeenth century scenes of daily life – genre subjects – came into fashion. In the past such material was to be found with rare exception only in the cheaper media of woodcuts and engravings. This double portrait is essentially a genre picture. A young girl and her duenna stare boldly at the spectator, much as Murillo must have seen such women gazing from the high windows in the narrow streets of Seville. The painting was popularly known as *Las Gallegas*, the Galicians, referring to the tradition that it represents two notorious courtesans of Seville who originally came from the province of Galicia. Murillo was an artist of the people: genial, commonplace in outlook, with an easy eloquence. In religious painting his sentiment was torrential, and his immense popularity finally wore away a technical ability which was second only to that of Velázquez. Disconcertingly uneven as was his achievement, he occasionally created a masterpiece like the present picture. Here he has avoided the sticky sentimentality and trite picturesqueness which spoil so much of his work. He presents these two prostitutes with that detached observation which is the hallmark of the best Spanish painting.

What Northern artist would have treated the subject with such subtle restraint? Rembrandt alone would have had the insight to eliminate the extraneous and focus attention, as Murillo has done, on the young girl so beautifully placed in the window, so plastically rendered. But not even Frans Hals would have had sufficient alertness of vision to suggest the smile of the older woman, witty, sardonic, yet expressed by the eyes and cheek alone. Collections: Duque de Almodóvar, Madrid; Lord Heytesbury, Heytesbury House, Wiltshire. *Widener Collection,* 1942. Painted c.1670.

155

PETER PAUL RUBENS (Flemish, 1577–1640)   Canvas
Isabella Brant
Catalogue No. 47   Height 60¼" (153 cm.) Width 47¼" (120 cm.)

In spite of the smiling face of the sitter there is about this portrait an elusive sadness. Isabella Brant was Rubens' first wife. They were married for fifteen years. She was painted by her husband many times, and these portraits reveal the gradual change from a buxom girl to a sick, middle-aged woman. The last of the series may be the portrait reproduced, which shows a face drawn and pinched by illness, though still with a courageous if somewhat wistful smile. In the background is the ornamental gateway which formed a part of the garden of Rubens' house in Antwerp, an entrance into what was once for Isabella her desirable life. But now her melancholy eyes seem to meditate on something else. Perhaps on the transience of beauty. Rubens seems to have loved her dearly.

In the eighteenth century the portrait reproduced was in the famous Crozat Collection where Watteau and many of his contemporaries learned to paint by copying Rubens and other artists. It was bought subsequently by Catherine the Great for the Hermitage Gallery in Leningrad. In recent years a number of critics have suggested that the painting may be by van Dyck. They tend to identify it with the picture which Félibien, writing in 1666, says van Dyck gave to his master on leaving his studio as a token of gratitude. Collections: Crozat, Paris; Catherine II, Empress of Russia; Hermitage Gallery, Leningrad. *Mellon Collection,* 1937. Painted between 1623 and 1626, the year Isabella died.

PETER PAUL RUBENS (Flemish, 1577–1640)   Wood
The Meeting of Abraham and Melchizedek
Catalogue No. 1506   Height 26" (66 cm.) Width 32½" (82.5 cm.)

The Infanta Isabella, widow of Archduke Albert of Austria, commissioned Rubens to design a series of tapestries illustrating the Triumph of the Eucharist. Since the bread and wine offered to Abraham by Melchizedek prefigure the Eucharist, the Old Testament scene was appropriately included in the series. The tapestries were woven in Brussels and are still in the Convent of the Poor Clares in Madrid to which the Infanta presented them in 1628. As the painting reproduced is more finished in composition and in execution than most of Rubens' sketches, it may well have been the model which the artist presented to Isabella to give her a definite idea of what to

Continued on page 164

156

SIR ANTHONY VAN DYCK (Flemish, 1599–1641)
MARCHESA ELENA GRIMALDI,
WIFE OF MARCHESE NICOLA CATTANEO   Canvas
Catalogue No. 686   Height 97″ (246 cm.)
                                            Width 68″ (173 cm.)

Paintings have their vicissitudes, as do human beings. Van Dyck's portrait
of the Marchesa Elena Grimaldi has experienced the mutability of fortune.
It was probably painted in 1623 when the artist was a young man, still at
the height of his vigor. He had left his native Flanders and settled tem-
porarily in Genoa where he became overnight the fashionable portraitist
of the patrician families. There he created on canvas a race of supermen
and women, richly dressed, of lofty stature and aloof expression. However,
of all the Genoese who sat for him, van Dyck has given to none so digni-
fied, so majestic a pose as to the wife of the Marchese Cattaneo. He has
also favored her with perhaps his most brilliant design. How skillfully the
parasol is used to heighten still further the Marchesa's tallness, 'towering
in her pride of place,' as she advances across her terrace and casts at the
spectator, far below, an appraising glance! This is the ultimate in the grand
manner in portraiture.

The failure of their trade and the decline of their independence, however, brought the great families of Genoa close to destitution. Early in this
century when the van Dyck scholar, Lionel Cust, gained admission to the
Cattaneo palace, he was ushered into a room where he halted spellbound.
'From every wall, as it seemed, Van Dyck looked down, and on one there
stood and gazed at me a haughty dame, over whose head a negro-page held
a scarlet parasol. All, however, spoke of dust and neglect, and when I left
the palace, it was with a feeling of regret that such treasures of painting
should be left to moulder on the walls.' Van Dyck's masterworks were not
to crumble away much longer; they had in fact reached the nadir of their
fortune. A dealer bought all the Cattaneo paintings shortly before the First
World War, and eventually Mr P. A. B. Widener acquired the most important of the lot, the portrait of the Marchesa Grimaldi and the portrait
of her two children (page 270). Collections: Palazzo Cattaneo, Genoa.
Widener Collection, 1942. Painted probably 1623.

FRANS HALS (Dutch, c. 1580–1666)

BALTHASAR COYMANS   Canvas
Catalogue No. 69   Height 30¹/₄″ (77 cm.)
                                                Width 25″ (64 cm.)

Frans Hals is an artist difficult to evaluate. There is more truth in one of
his portraits than in a gallery of portraits by van Dyck. But what sitter
really wants truth in portraiture? As Fromentin wrote, van Dyck was
'admired everywhere, invited everywhere, welcomed everywhere ... the
equal of the greatest lords, the favorite and friend of kings.' Frans Hals
died in the poorhouse. And yet we feel that this is not as shocking as it
might be, for he was not among the greatest portraitists. The truth of
characterization in his paintings was fundamentally superficial. We know
Balthasar Coymans as we might know someone on shipboard who passes
our deck-chairs daily but whom we never meet. Was he really as jaunty
as all that? Was he proud of his coat of arms which enables us to identify
him *(koey* means 'cow,' therefore, *koeymans* or 'the cowman')? What was
he really like?

The archives tell us that Balthasar Coymans (1618–1690) was Lord of
Streefkerk and Nieuw Lekkerland and an Alderman of Haarlem. We recognize how, with a seemingly dissipated tilt of his hat, Hals has given
this important citizen the appearance of a common rake. It occurs to us
that Hals was in a way an inverted alchemist. The gold we all believe lies
in our personality he transformed with his brush into its true lead. But
then we are struck by the pyrotechnics of his brush. With what genius he
controls its swordplay! How far above his imitators he remained, artists
like Duveneck and Sargent, to name two! How unique was his magic
staccato touch which rendered the objects with a few brilliant strokes!
Those of us who love painting for its own sake will find more delight in
the sleeve and collar of Coymans' shirt than in all the paint-ennobled
aristocracy of Sir Anthony van Dyck. Collections: Coymans family,
Haarlem; Mrs Frederick Wollaston, London; Rodolphe Kann, Paris; Mrs
Collis P. Huntington, New York; Archer E. Huntington, New York.
Mellon Collection, 1937. Dated 1645.

REMBRANDT VAN RYN (Dutch, 1606–1669)   Canvas

The Mill

Catalogue No. 658   Height 34½″ (87.5 cm.) Width 41½″ (105.5 cm.)

The Mill is Rembrandt's supreme achievement in landscape painting. It is usually dated about 1650, when he was still at the height of his fame. John Constable judged it 'sufficient to form an epoch in the art ... the first picture in which a sentiment has been expressed by chiaroscuro only, all details being excluded.' And this melancholy sentiment, this mood of sublime sadness, which Rembrandt conveys through the stark simplicity of a windmill silhouetted in the fading light against the mist-filled sky, is indescribably moving.

Probably no single canvas has so strongly affected English painting. Turner admired it and the notes in his sketchbook show that it was the basis of his conception of Rembrandt's handling of light. Sir Joshua Reynolds painted a free adaptation of it; and it was engraved by Charles Turner for his *Gems of Art*, a book to be found in the studio of nearly every nineteenth-century English painter. Collections: Duc d'Orléans, Paris; William Smith, London; Marquess of Lansdowne, Bowood Hall, Wiltshire. *Widener Collection*, 1942. Painted c. 1650.

REMBRANDT VAN RYN (Dutch, 1606–1669)   Canvas

Joseph Accused by Potiphar's Wife

Catalogue No. 79   Height 41⅝″ (106 cm.) Width 38½″ (98 cm.)

This picture is a calmer, more monumental version of the subject treated in another picture in the Berlin Museum, which is also dated 1655. Joseph is falsely accused by Phraxanor, the wife of Potiphar, of trying to seduce her. The reverse is actually the case, as the story is told in Genesis 39. The scene was one which Baroque artists were delighted to represent. Usually Joseph is shown fleeing from his would-be seductress, who leaps from her bed and grabs at his coat, here shown on the bedpost. But Rembrandt has treated the story at the level of highest tragedy. The aging beauty, the beautiful youth, the puzzled husband, all seem bemused by passions beyond their comprehension. One senses Rembrandt's deep compassion for each of the actors in this archetypal domestic drama. Had this scene of frustrated passion, one wonders, any special significance for its former owner, Catherine the Great of Russia, who seems so often to have fallen in love with men younger than herself? Collections: Catherine II, Empress of Russia; Hermitage Gallery, Leningrad. *Mellon Collection*, 1937. Signed, and dated 1655 (the last cipher is unclear).

REMBRANDT VAN RYN (Dutch, 1606–1669)   Canvas
SELF-PORTRAIT
Catalogue No. 72   Height 33¼″ (84 cm.)   Width 26″ (66 cm.)

Rembrandt was a much more profound artist than Frans Hals. Few auto-
biographies are as searching as his self-portraits. The one reproduced was
signed and dated 1659, ten years before his death. In 1656 he had been
declared bankrupt and during the next two years everything he owned was
sold. His son and his mistress were shortly to make themselves custodians
even of his still-unpainted pictures. Society had judged him and had declared him incompetent. Once more he looked in a mirror to take stock
of himself, to analyze the problem of his personality. He saw reflected a
face lined with age and misfortune. He saw eyes which had searched more
profoundly into the human soul than those of any other artist. He saw a
mouth and a chin weak, infirm of purpose, manifesting that flaw in his
character which had ruined his life. His hands are grasped as though in
anguish at the spectacle of a self-ruined man. There exists no painting more
pitiless in its analysis or more pitiful in its implications. Collections: Duke
of Buccleuch, London. *Mellon Collection,* 1937. Signed, and dated 1659.

Continued from page 156
expect in the final appearance of the series Rubens apparently made a
particular effort over this subject, for there is a drawing in the Albertina
in Vienna, a grisaille sketch in the Fitzwilliam Museum in Cambridge, England, and the color sketch in the Prado, in Madrid.

His efforts were rewarded, for he conveys here, as brilliantly as in any
of his works, the special qualities of his genius. First, there is that spiritual
exuberance we associate with the Counter Reformation, superbly expressed
in the sustained rhythm of twisting and turning figures, all designed to
intensify the dramatic effect. Then there is the extraordinary transmutation
of the pigment itself, which becomes flesh, fur, silk, and steel while remain-
ing paint, a miraculous change Rubens could work as no other artist. And
last there is that amassment of rich materials to create a sumptuousness
which was the goal of all Baroque decorators, among whom Rubens was
supreme. Collections: Jean de Jullienne, Paris; J. B. Horion, Brussels; Lady
Stuart, London; Sir Thomas Baring, London; Lord Northbrook, London;
Walter Stoye, Oxford. *Gift of Syma Busiel,* 1958. Painted c. 1625.

JAN VERMEER (Dutch, 1633–1675)
A WOMAN WEIGHING GOLD   Canvas
Catalogue No. 693   Height 16³/₄" (42.5 cm.)
                                                  Width 15" (38 cm.)

Jan Vermeer of Delft was a master of stillness, of those moments of life
when all action has ceased, held by an ephemeral adjustment of forces. The
canvas in the National Gallery of Art conveys this sense of dynamic quies-
cence; it is in fact an allegory of balances. The unmoving figure weighing
gold balances in her scales her earthly treasure, while Christ in the Last
Judgment in the background, in His divine knowledge weighs human guilt.
The woman is absorbed, wrapped in the serene and mysterious thought of
approaching maternity; and her pregnant body half concealing the painting hung behind her suggests a further equation, as though, as in Santayana's
phrase, 'The truth of life could be seen only in the shadow of death; living
and dying were simultaneous and inseparable.'

Such symbolic profundity is rare among Dutch painters of the seventeenth century and only intermittent in Vermeer's own work. The quality
for which his paintings are always distinguished is form rather than content.
For Vermeer among all Dutch artists is unrivaled in his mastery of optical
reality. In his paintings just so much detail is included as can be seen from
a normal distance, not by focusing the eye successively on different objects,
nor in an instant of time, but with a steady gaze. Similarly in his treatment
of tone relations, there is a perfect consistency with what we actually see.
No other painter has been able to maintain such subtle distinctions of color
in different planes of light, nor to extend this organization of tone into
such depths of shadow. Collections: Possibly in the collection of Jac.
Abrahamsz. Dissius, Amsterdam; Nieuhof, Amsterdam; van der Bogaerd,
Amsterdam; King of Bavaria, Munich; Duke of Caraman, Vienna and
Paris; Casimir Périer; Countess de Ségur (née Périer), Paris. *Widener Col-
lection*, 1942. Painted c. 1657.

JAN VERMEER (Dutch, 1632–1675)
YOUNG GIRL WITH A FLUTE   Wood
Catalogue No. 694   Height 7⅞" (20 cm.)
                                           Width 7" (18 cm.)

The total number of pictures by Vermeer numbers roughly forty. Of these, two of the most beautiful are *The Girl with a Red Hat* (page 275) and *Young Girl with a Flute*. These two paintings, which Vermeer must have intended to hang together since the same tapestried background and the same chair appear in both, were separated in the seventeenth century, only to be reunited in the twentieth, when Mr Mellon gave one to the National Gallery and Mr Widener the other. The height of the *Young Girl with a Flute* has been slightly reduced, and it is still apparent where the panel was cut down.

Both pictures are superb examples of Vermeer's characteristic technique, which is most evident in works like these when he used wood as a support. Here one sees clearly how much more vitreous the surface is than in other Dutch paintings, with the pigments seemingly fused in a glassy medium. It has been suggested that this is the result of painting from images reflected in a mirror. But the hat of the young girl, calling to mind as it does some Chinese origin, implies another explanation. Delft, where Vermeer worked, was closely in contact with the Orient because of its famous china. The paintings on Chinese porcelains have a vitreous look, and craftsmen in Delft studied how to imitate this effect. Is it not possible that Vermeer was seeking to achieve on wood and canvas something of the surface texture of Chinese porcelain painting? The only other artist, so far as I know, who gained a similar effect in his pictures is the English painter George Stubbs. And we know Stubbs worked for a famous porcelain manufacturer, Josiah Wedgewood. This may be a coincidence, but if not, it would seem to throw some light on the mystery of Vermeer's technical method. Collections: Possibly Jac. Abrahamsz. Dissius, Amsterdam; Jan Mahie van Boxtel en Liempde; 's-Hertogenbosch, Holland; de Grez family, Brussels; August Janssen, Amsterdam. *Widener Collection*, 1942. Painted c. 1658–1660.

GERARD TER BORCH (Dutch, 1617–1681)

THE SUITOR'S VISIT

Catalogue No. 58

Canvas

Height 31½" (80 cm.)

Width 29⅝" (75 cm.)

The easel picture, the kind of picture we are accustomed to hang in our homes, flourished in the seventeenth century, especially in Calvinistic Holland. Here a new secular style replaced the timeless dramas of Christian art, which had occupied painters in the past; and instead momentary glimpses of everyday life became the fashion. Of such genre pieces *The Suitor's Visit* is typical. We watch, as though through an open window, the suitor in all his finery forever approaching his pensive fiancée; while her father from behind looks on appraisingly, and her sister or friend with self-conscious concentration strums on a theorbo. As sometimes happens in the movies, the film seems to have caught, the actors suddenly to have become immobile. Everyone, even the dog, questions the future which cannot begin while the enchanted stillness lasts. Here is a different kind of timelessness, one described by Goethe when he said to Eckermann, 'Every situation – nay, every moment – is of infinite worth; for it is the representative of a whole eternity.'

This new search in painting for the permanent in the ephemeral led to a more realistic transcription of appearance. The achievement of this neccessitates a careful adjustment of tones and values. In the present picture the figure of the suitor, the friend, and the father are mutually consistent, but the figure of the fiancée is out of key. The highlights on her white dress and coral bodice are too bright to be justified by the apparent illumination of the room. This overemphasis on certain passages, especially of white silk, repeatedly upsets the balance of ter Borch's colors. Yet paradoxially his fame rests on this flaw in the actuality of his scenes, for the popularity of his canvases is due largely to his handling of satin, to his rendering of texture which, skillful as it is, at the same time affects the reality of his paintings. Collections: Charles-Auguste-Louis-Joseph, Duc de Morny, Paris; Marqués de Salamanca, Madrid; Adolphe de Rothschild, Paris; Maurice de Rothschild, Paris. *Mellon Collection,* 1937. Painted c.1658.

PIETER DE HOOCH (Dutch, 1629–1683)
A Dutch Courtyard   Canvas
Catalogue No. 56   Height 26³/₄″ (68 cm.)
                                            Width 23″ (59 cm.)

Paul Claudel, the French poet, has analyzed with wonderful penetration
the charm of Dutch scenes of everyday life such as the picture reproduced.
He points out that these canvases make us conscious of time. 'They are the
reservoir of evanescent feelings. We do not merely glance at a painting
by ... de Hooch with condescending approval; we are immediately within
it, we live there.' Thus, as in paintings by Vermeer and ter Borch, we
share an ephemeral moment which is given an enchanted permanence.

   Beyond the wall of de Hooch's courtyard is the Nieuwe Kerk in Delft.
This picture was probably painted, therefore, when during the 1650s
de Hooch was living in the native city of the greatest of the Dutch genre
painters, Jan Vermeer. During several years under the inspiration of Vermeer, he painted, along with his more unusual interiors, an occasional scene
out-of-doors. In these he catches in a web of almost invisible brush strokes
the texture of crumbling brick and mortar, the undulations of old paving,
the gleam of metals, and the transparency of liquids. Masterpieces of a true
visual effect, such canvases conjure up a domestic paradise of eternal, sun-
drenched felicity. The best painters in Holland, with the exception of
Rembrandt, were in varying degrees scientific investigators of such images
which the eye conveys to the mind. It is significant in this connection that
the Dutch are also credited with the practical discovery of both the com-
pound microscope and the telescope, one in 1590, and the other in 1608.
Collections: Possibly Samuel A. Koopman, Utrecht; Baron Lionel Nathan
de Rothschild; Alfred Charles de Rothschild; Countess of Carnarvon,
Newbury, England. *Mellon Collection,* 1937. Painted c.1660. Another version, lacking the cavalier holding the beer jug, is in the Mauritshuis, The
Hague (formerly Ten Cate Collection).

JACOB VAN RUISDAEL (Dutch, 1628/29–1682)   Canvas
FOREST SCENE   Height 41¹/₂″ (105.5 cm.) Width 51¹/₂″ (131 cm.)
Catalogue No. 676

The Dutch landscape, judged by itself, rarely reaches an exalted place in
the hierarchy of painting. But from the viewpoint of the development of
the representation of nature, it is almost as important in modern art as is
Byzantine painting in the history of Christian art.

This realistic attitude toward nature appears in all the paintings by
Ruisdael; but he also tried to convey an emotional response to the scene.
In Claude's pictures an emotional reaction to landscape is suggested by a
kind of stage scenery; in Ruisdael's canvases nature is shown in its everyday
appearance. Claude recalls Vergil; Ruisdael, Wordsworth. One evokes an
Arcadian world, conveying to the spectator a corresponding tranquility of
spirit; the other creates a totally different mood, either one of loneliness
and foreboding before the tangled darkness of encroaching forests, or of
exultation at distant vistas of land and water under a cold and sullen sky.
Collections: Sir Hugh Hume Campbell, Berwickshire. *Widener Collection,*
1942. Signed. Painted c. 1660–65.

AELBERT CUYP (Dutch, 1620–1691)
THE MAAS AT DORDRECHT   Canvas
Catalogue No. 501   Height 45¹/₄″ (115 cm.)   Width 67″ (170 cm.)

Cuyp's animal paintings are rarely as fine as his less well known
pictures of the Dutch estuaries, such as the painting reproduced, where
reflected color and a broadly handled detail combine to create a masterpiece of visual truth. The aim of such paintings is portraiture, the exact
appearance of the Dutch harbors filled with shipping and men-of-war. To
criticize painters like Aelbert Cuyp, Jan van de Cappelle, and Willem van
de Velde because the calmer aspect of the sea is almost invariably shown,
is to mistake their purpose, for portraiture presupposes that the object
portrayed will remain relatively still.

On May 24, 1660, the boat carrying King Charles II of England, who,
during the period of the Commonwealth had resided for some time in
Breda, lay at anchor before Dordrecht before proceeding to The Hague
and thence back to England. This is the event which, according to Hans
Schneider, in all likelihood inspired the composition of *The Maas at Dordrecht.* Collections: Alexis de la Hante; Sir Abraham Hume, and his descendants, England. *Mellon Collection,* 1940. Signed. Painted c. 1660.

175

JAN DAVIDSZ. DE HEEM (Dutch, 1606–1683/84)

Vase of Flowers   Canvas

Catalogue No. 1649   Height 27³/₈" (69.6 cm.)

Width 22¹/₄" (56.5 cm.)

If one were to choose a single picture to summarize the achievement of Dutch and Flemish flower painting it might well be the picture reproduced. Executed at the apogee of seventeenth-century still-life painting, it combines the strength of earlier work with an added elegance and technical virtuosity. In the generation to follow, elegance becomes ornamentalism; virtuosity, display.

Of this middle generation of still-life painters, de Heem is considered the most influential. He was born in Holland, spent his early years in Utrecht and Leiden, and moved south to Antwerp in 1636. Receptive to the current styles of both northern and southern Netherlands, he synthesized them into a new style of his own which was to set the pattern of the decorative flowerpiece for the rest of the seventeenth century and far into the eighteenth, and which was to spread to France, Italy, and Spain.

This *Vase of Flowers,* however, does more than summarize an historical style. It survives for us as a brilliant solution of the problem of combining profusion and control. Not restricted to a variety of flowers, the picture includes vegetables and insects and reptiles, as well. Each detail, furthermore, has been painted with a desire for scientific exactitude, down to the last hair on the bumblebee's back. The colors, too, set off as they are against a luminous dark ground, and much more saturated than in de Heem's earlier works, add to the sense of richness.

But for all the painting's harmony, it is not without a vaguely sinister uneasiness. Partly this comes from the asymmetry of the arrangement, partly from the hidden insects, and from intimations of decay in the fallen poppy or the broken wheatstalk. De Heem, when he lived at the university town of Leiden, had been exposed to the tradition of *Vanitas* still-life painting centered there, which stressed through symbols the vanity and transitoriness of life on earth. Flowers, particularly cut flowers, with the morning dew still clinging to them, epitomized the evanescent. Collections: Baron Edmond de Rothschild; McIntosh, Bridge of Allan, Scotland. *National Gallery of Art Purchase Fund, Andrew W. Mellon Gift,* 1961. Signed. Painted c.1645.

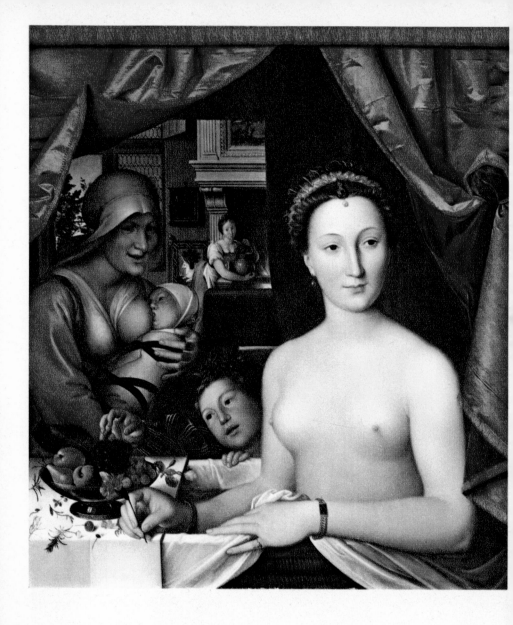

FRANÇOIS CLOUET (French, c. 1510–1572)
'DIANE DE POITIERS'   Wood
Catalogue No. 1370   Height 36¹/₄″ (92.1 cm.)
                                                       Width 32″ (81.3 cm.)

In the case of this masterpiece, one of two paintings signed by François
Clouet, we can rely only on tradition for the suggestion that it represents
Diane de Poitiers, one of the most remarkable women in French history.

Married at fifteen, Diane later became the mistress of Henry II, twenty
years her junior. Every morning she rose at six, took a cold bath and rode
horseback for two or three hours. She never used cosmetics; yet, according
to the Venetian ambassador, she looked at least fifteen to twenty years
younger than she was. Another account added, 'Her neck was full and
her shoulders well rounded; her mouth tight lipped and drawn in, seemed
made not to be kissed but to keep a secret; no softness, nor voluptuousness,
the air of a Roman Juno added to the gravity of a Venetian patrician.'

This portrait's setting may seem unusual, but Clouet made it popular at
the court of Fontainebleau. The curtains are drawn back, and Diane (if it
is she), sits in her bath without embarrassment at the intrusion. But one
must remember that during the Renaissance a bath was not the private
affair it is today. It was a luxury to be enjoyed to the utmost, and com-
panionship added to the pleasure. Surrounding the bather are children and
servants. A little boy reaches for fruit, a baby is suckled by a wet-nurse.
In the background a maid is ready to replenish the bath with water,
probably perfumed. Beyond the maid is a chair with the tapestry back
showing a unicorn, ancient symbol of chastity – a tribute perhaps not
entirely justified if the bather is to be identified as Diane de Poitiers. Collections: Sir Richard Frederick, Burwood Park; Cook, Doughty House,
Richmond, Surrey. *Samuel H. Kress Collection*, 1955. Signed. Painted
probably c. 1571; the lady's coiffure is identical in style to that of Clouet's
portrait of Elizabeth of Austria, in the Louvre, a drawing for which is
dated 1571.

CLAUDE LORRAIN (French, 1600–1682)   Canvas
THE HERDSMAN
Catalogue No. 784   Height 47³/₄″ (121.5 cm)   Width 63¹/₈″ (160.5 cm.)

Claude Lorrain was the supreme master of the classical interpretation of
nature. The picture reproduced might have been painted to illustrate Book
III of Vergil' *Georgics*. The hill from which the scene is viewed; the masses
of shadow in the foreground; the schematized foliage in silhouette with no
branch coming toward the spectator: all these devices are used to enframe
the vista, to enhance the effect of those continuously receding planes that
draw the spectator deep into the landscape.

From the sweep of space in his paintings, from the way the eye glides to
distant mountains and headlands, clear in shape but impalpable in substance, comes a curious psychological release – an emotion difficult to define
but one which makes Claude, for some of us, the most satisfactory of all
landscape painters. Collections: Baron Gustave de Rothschild, Paris; Marquess of Cholmondeley, Houghton Hall, Norfolk, England. *Samuel H.
Kress Collection*, 1945. Painted probably 1655–60.

NICOLAS POUSSIN (French, 1593/94–1665)   Canvas
HOLY FAMILY ON THE STEPS
Catalogue No. 1128   Height 27″ (68.6 cm.) Width 38¹/₂″ (97.8 cm.)

Poussin defined the grand manner of painting as consisting of four elements,
which he declared were, 'subject matter or theme, thought, structure, and
style. The first thing that, as the foundation of all others, is required,' he
said, 'is that the subject matter shall be grand.

The *Holy Family on the Steps* perfectly illustrates Poussin's theory. It
is of a divine subject; the thought is lofty; the structure is skillfully arranged; and the style shows Poussin's particular gift. It is one of the most
beautiful compositions he ever achieved – a challenge to Raphael, with a
complex richness of form in the relation between the pyramidal group of
figures and the geometrical shapes of the architecture, which Raphael never
attempted in his easel pictures and attained only in the frescoes of the
Stanze in the Vatican. Note how the asymmetrical placing of the bowl,
the jar, and the box, serves to balance the design. Collections: Nicolas
Hannequin, Baron d'Ecquevilly, Sieur de Fresne; Hôtel de Guise, Paris
(presumably in the collection of François-Roger de Caignières); Abbé Le-
blanc; Duke of Sutherland, Stafford House, London. *Samuel H. Kress
Collection*, 1949. Painted 1648.

LOUIS LE NAIN (French, c. 1593–1648)   Canvas
LANDSCAPE WITH PEASANTS
Catalogue No. 783   Height 18³/₈" (46.5 cm.)   Width 22¹/₂" (57 cm.)

Louis Le Nain has caught the exact tone of that gray northern light so characteristic of the countryside near the Belgian border. This feeling for a particular place gives his picture a modern quality.

The three Le Nain brothers, all painters, were apparently trained by a Dutch artist. Their work represented a reaction against the academic style, discussed in connection with Poussin's *Holy Family* (page 181). Poussin seems to have had them in mind when he said, 'Those who elect mean subjects take refuge in them because of the weakness of their talents.' It is evident that the Le Nain brothers were disliked by the official court painters led by Poussin, who were occupied with religious themes or scenes of history or mythology. But there was a demand among middle-class patrons for glimpses of rural life, a demand which the three brothers helped satisfy with the canvases they exhibited and sold at popular fairs, such as those at St Germain-des-Prés.   *Continued on page 192*

ANTOINE WATTEAU (French, 1684–1721)   Canvas
ITALIAN COMEDIANS
Catalogue No. 774   Height 25¹/₈" (64 cm.)   Width 30" (76 cm.)

In the eighteenth century the most creative school of painting was in France. Watteau was the founder of French eighteenth-century painting, of a style of art which dominated European taste. The *Italian Comedians*, painted the year before he died at the age of thirty-seven, was one of his last important undertakings. The young painter was already consumptive. He had traveled to England early in 1720 in the hope of improving his fortune and recovering his health. Once there, his illness increased, and he consulted a leading physician of the time, Dr Richard Mead. But there was nothing to be done and he returned to France. Either in London or in Paris he painted for his doctor and new friend this canvas of the *Italian Comedians*, a famous troupe who had been disbanded in 1697 on orders of Madame de Maintenon but who had been allowed to resume their plays in 1716. From contemporary accounts it now seems evident that Watteau did not paint the actors themselves but posed his acquaintances in the costumes of these mimes. Pierrot or Gilles who stands in the center, for
Continued on page 195

FRANÇOIS BOUCHER (French, 1703-1770)
VENUS CONSOLING LOVE   Canvas
Catalogue No. 739   Height 42¹/₈" (107 cm.)
                                             Width 33³/₈" (85 cm.)

Melancholy, however, was a rare quality in the eighteenth century,
especially in France. Such overtones of sadness never appear in the
paintings of Boucher. *Venus Consoling Love* once belonged to Madame
de Pompadour. It is signed and dated 1751, the year Louis XV's mistress
moved into a new apartment in the north wing of Versailles, where she
was to live the rest of her life. It may have adorned these rooms or else
have been painted for her château at Bellevue, where Boucher was working
around 1750. He was Madame de Pompadour's favorite artist. She gave
him commissions for innumerable decorations and easel pictures; ordered
from him an illuminated prayer book, surprising as such a commission must
seem; petted and cajoled him; and wrote her counselor of state that he
must be kept in a good humor. For as she said, 'I'm sure you would hate
to find a crippled or cock-eyed nymph in your pretty room.'

Madame de Pompadour has been said to have posed for the Venus in
the painting reproduced. But this entrancing maiden is much more the
product of the painter's imagination. Boucher was never tied down to a
model. He had learned a language of design, and this he used with the
utmost freedom. Notice with what grace the movement of Venus, Cupid,
and the surrounding putti is suggested. Or notice the lovely passages of
painting in the feathers of the dove, the flowers, and the foliage. Eighteenth-century painters delighted in the display of beautiful handling, of
fine brushwork, much as a violinist might take pleasure in a virtuoso performance. In this technical dexterity lies the principal charm of Rococo
art. Collections: Mme de Pompadour; Marquis de Ménars; H. Cousin;
Baron Alfred de Rothschild, Buckingham, England; Marchioness of Cur-
zon, Kedleston, Derbyshire. *Gift of Chester Dale,* 1943. Signed, and dated
1751.

JEAN-BAPTISTE-SIMEON CHARDIN (French, 1699–1779)

THE ATTENTIVE NURSE   Canvas
Catalogue No. 1116   Height 18¹/₈″ (46.2 cm.)
                                                  Width 14¹/₂″ (37 cm.)

Boucher was the favorite of Madame de Pompadour; Chardin, of Diderot. The mistress of the king and the editor of the Encyclopedia had different tastes: one wished to see on canvas the enticements of femininity, the other the virtues of domesticity. In the long run feminine charm is more tedious than domestic virtue, especially when this virtue is interpreted by Chardin's brush, which gilds with poetic light the everyday life of the middle class in eighteenth-century France.

For it was Chardin's talent to find plastic poetry in a bowl of fruit, a blue-and-white pitcher, or a nurse preparing a meal for her convalescent patient. In the picture reproduced the painter conveys, with his exquisite sensibility, emotions of love and tenderness, sincere feelings springing from the charity in his heart but difficult to express without banality and triteness. Nothing could be further from the sometimes delicious and always glittering artificiality preferred at Versailles. Chardin was a product of Paris – the city of merchants and bankers, of traders and shopkeepers, of encyclopedists and bluestockings. His art is an affirmation of their independently-developed taste, which at its best has a great appeal. But it was also a taste in which was latent that germ of sentimentality which a hundred years later became a plague and almost destroyed French painting.

Chardin's canvases also had considerable charm for the aristocracy. *The Attentive Nurse* was purchased from the artist by the Prince of Liechtenstein when he was Austrian Ambassador to France. Being one of the few works by Chardin which were not engraved before being sold, it has been assumed that the Prince was so enamored of the picture, when it was displayed in the Salon of 1747, that he took it immediately to Vienna. Apart from a sketch which was probably the basis for Jules de Goncourt's etching, there are no other versions, which is unusual in Chardin's genre compositions of this type. Collections: The Princes of Liechtenstein. *Samuel H. Kress Collection,* 1950. Signed. Painted probably 1738, the date which appears on its pendant, *The Governess,* in the National Gallery of Canada, Ottawa.

JEAN-HONORÉ FRAGONARD (French, 1732–1806)
A YOUNG GIRL READING   Canvas
Catalogue No. 1653   Height 32" (81.1 cm.)
                                                Width 25½" (64.8 cm.)

Painted about 1776 at the peak of the artist's career, this charming study
is considered by many critics to be among Fragonard's most appealing and
masterly paintings. It is one of a series representing young girls in moments
of solitude and relaxation, either reading a billet-doux, turning the pages
of a book, or seated at a dressing table and lost in the world of their
private thoughts. The identity of the sitters, as in this case, is unknown.
Apparently Fragonard painted this series on speculation, hoping to interest
Parisian patrons who were decorating their private apartments with
intimate scenes typical of the last phase of Rococo taste.

Few paintings reveal more brilliantly that wonderful dexterity of brushwork, for which Fragonard was famous. Look first at the curving fingers
of the girl's hand holding the book. These fingers establish a rhythm which
runs through the whole painting. The same movement, to be seen in various
brush strokes is especially noticeable in the delicate and complicated
touches which render the bows, the ribbons, and the ruffles of the young
girl's costume. As in Boucher's *Venus Consoling Love* (see p. 185) the
quality of this brushwork has a spontaneity suggestive of a Mozartian
cadenza. This virtuoso performance reaches a climax in the broad strokes
of burnt umber, which model the cushion and suggest its softly-yielding
volume. All these warm tones, placed so rapidly on the canvas, seem aglow
with sunshine. Collections: Leroy de Senneville, Paris; Duquesnoy, Paris;
Marquis de Cypierre, Paris; Comte de Kergorlay, Paris; Ernest Cronier,
Paris; Dr Tuffier, Paris; Mr and Mrs Alfred W. Erickson, New York.
*Gift of Mrs Mellon Bruce in memory of her father Andrew W. Mellon,
1961. Painted c. 1776.*

188

GIOVANNI BATTISTA TIEPOLO (Venetian, 1696–1770)

MADONNA OF THE GOLDFINCH   Canvas

Catalogue No. 541   Height 24⁷/₈″ (63 cm.)

Width 19³/₄″ (50 cm.)

Tiepolo was not only the last of the great decorators, he was also among the last of the great religious painters. With the end of the eighteenth century, religion, which had been steadily declining as an inspiration to art, all but disappeared from significant painting. From the death of Tiepolo until today it is difficult to name a single artist who has shown more than a sporadic ability to create satisfactory devotional pictures, whether altarpieces or easel paintings.

Canvases like the *Madonna of the Goldfinch*, therefore, take on an added interest as examples of the end of one phase of Christian art. In looking at Tiepolo's religious paintings one is struck immediately by the physical charm of the figures and at the same time by the aloof, almost disdainful character of their beauty. It is this expression of reserve, of detachment, which gives to his Madonna and her Child, a dignity that contrasts strikingly with the cloying allurement apparent in almost every modern treatment of this theme. Yet the attraction of what is merely pretty is perilously close, even in Tiepolo. It is ennobled by the treatment of the figures, by the innate superiority, the unapproachable reserve Tiepolo has given them, and also by the virtuosity of brushwork, drawing, and color; but it is there, nevertheless, a portent of the precipitous decline from the sublime to the meretricious which was to be the fate of Italian painting, a fate that only Tiepolo's genius was able to delay. The center of European culture was moving from the Mediterranean northward, and shortly after Tiepolo's death Italy, like Spain a few years later, was destined to lose touch with the main movements of art. Collections: Principe del Drago, Rome; Arthur Maier, Karlsbad. *Samuel H. Kress Collection,* 1940. Painted c. 1760.

191

THOMAS GAINSBOROUGH (British, 1727–1788)   Canvas
Mrs Richard Brinsley Sheridan
Catalogue No. 92   Height 86½″ (220 cm.) Width 60½″ (154 cm.)

To understand this portrait one must remember its background in Whig society of the late eighteenth century – a society materialistic, rich, self-confident, yet with a love of learning, freedom, and a special sensibility that sometimes verged on sentimentality. Mrs Sheridan, the beautiful singer who married the wit, playwright, brilliant member of Parliament, and drunken favorite of Devonshire House, is a characteristic figure in that society. And this picture, at once charmingly pastoral (although nature is somewhat arranged, as the great Whig nobles liked it to be) and dashingly, artificially worldly, is a consummate expression of high Whig taste.

Gainsborough is known to have painted on occasion with brushes mounted on handles almost six feet long, in order to be the same distance from his model and his canvas. The consequent sketchiness of effect make the certainty of each brush stroke still more remarkable. This feature of his style impressed Sir Joshua Reynolds who wrote, 'This chaos, this uncouth and shapeless appearance, by a kind of magic, at a certain distance assumes form, and all the parts seem to drop into their proper places; so that we can hardly refuse acknowledging the full effect of diligence, under the appearance of chance and hasty negligence.' Collections: Richard Brinsley Sheridan, Bath, England; Baron Nathaniel de Rothschild, Tring, Hertfordshire and heirs until sold by Lord Rothschild, London. *Mellon Collection*, 1937. Painted probably 1785 – 86.

Continued from page 183
This picture is probably the canvas listed in the exhibition catalogue of Thomas Gainsborough's collection. The sweep of landscape, with its strongly emphasized receding planes, was exactly what Gainsborough sought in his early work, usually thought to be entirely under Dutch influence. Actually this continual recession, neither interrupted by detail nor broken up by bands of light and shade, is rare in Dutch art; and Gainsborough in his handling of distance in landscape seems also to owe a debt to France, which should not be ignored. Collections: Probably Thomas Gainsborough, London; Dr Didbin; Joseph Neeld, London; Sir Audley Neeld, Chippenham, Wiltshire. *Samuel H. Kress Collection*, 1945. Painted c. 1640.

192

Lady Caroline Howard
Lady Cawdor

SIR JOSHUA REYNOLDS (British, 1723–1792)   Canvas
LADY CAROLINE HOWARD
Catalogue No. 106   Height 56¹/₄″ (143 cm.) Width 44¹/₂″ (113 cm.)

In the portrait of Lady Caroline Howard, Reynolds has stressed a certain
aspect of childhood, its innocence, its unstudied gracefulness. It does not
matter that the portrait may not be a precise likeness of Lady Caroline,
nor even that he used a similar pose and setting in other paintings of
children, notably in *The Age of Innocence* in the National Gallery, London. For 'the great aim of the art,' as he said addressing the Royal Academy, 'is to strike the imagination.' In the portrait of Lady Caroline the
mind is captured and converted to the Romantic concept of childhood,
'trailing clouds of glory,' thirty years before Wordsworth's poem. Need-
less to say Reynolds himself was a bachelor!

Reynolds, in spite of the classical creed expounded in his *Discourses,*
proves himself in many ways a precursor of the Romantics. This is manifest
not only in his tendency to sentimentality, but also in his faltering technique, in that uncertainty of craftsmanship which was the plague of Romantic painting. Thus many of his canvases, because of his constant technical experiments and his constant use of bitumen, have cracked and faded.
Lady Caroline Howard, however, has lasted with its original brilliance
and freshness; and for that reason it gives an idea of the luminosity of tone
which must have characterized Reynold's portraits when they left his
studio, an impression hard to gain from most of his pictures in their present
condition. Collections: Earl of Carlisle, Castle Howard, England. *Mellon
Collection,* 1937. Painted c. 1778.

Continued from page 183
example, has been tentatively identified as Corneille van Clève, Rector of
the Royal Academy of Sculpture.

In many of Watteau's paintings we sense under their superficial mer-
riment a subtle melancholy. This elusive sadness permeates the *Italian
Comedians.* There is, indeed, something particularly moving about this
picture of gaiety painted by a dying artist for the doctor who had prob-
ably told him that he had only a short time to live. Collections: Dr Richard
Mead, London; Roger Harene, London; Sir Thomas Baring, London; Lord
Northbrook, London; Lord Iveagh, London; Walter Guinness, London;
Dr Heinrich Baron Thyssen-Bornemisza (Schloss Rohoncz), Villa Favorita,
Lugano. *Samuel H. Kress Collection,* 1945. Painted in 1720.

GEORGE ROMNEY (British, 1734–1802)
MISS WILLOUGHBY   Canvas
Catalogue No. 104   Height 36⅛″ (91 cm.)
                               Width 28″ (71 cm.)

If there were only a divining rod to point out those artists destined to be the Old Masters of the future, we might enjoy portraits of ourselves or our children and at the same time count on our descendants being copiously enriched. Miss Willoughby's parents in 1784 paid Romney less than one-thousandth part of the price his picture brought when it was acquired for the National Gallery of Art a few decades ago, and many families in Europe today owe their fortunes to the perspicacity with which their ancestors selected their portraitists.

But how can we tell what picture will gain in appreciation? Why has *Miss Willoughby,* for instance, come to be so highly treasured? It is merely the conventional and scarcely individualized portrait of a pretty child. Perhaps Romney was even bored with the commission, for he disliked portraiture, and the only sitter he seems to have taken pleasure in painting was Emma, Lady Hamilton, whose strange, restless magnetism enthralled and maddened him. When he painted other people his real interests lay in solving certain problems of color and design rather than in getting a likeness.

But then, who cares any longer what Miss Willoughby looked like? Her portrait is enjoyed today because of Romney's genius as a colorist and as a decorator. The harmonious tone of the picture is a lesson in the adroit use of a limited palette, in this case a palette of only three colors, red, yellow, and blue. The design is as simple as the color, but just as subtly ingenious. The gesture of the child seems spontaneous and unposed, but note the tilt of the head at just the right angle to suggest a diagonal movement crosscutting the diagonal of the sloping landscape in the background. Imagine it upright and the rhythm of the composition vanishes. And how satisfactory in scale is Miss Willoughby in relation to the canvas. These qualities of color and design, so frequently to be found in eighteenth-century English portraiture, are the antecedent facts which make it probable that a painting will continue to interest posterity. Collections: Major Sir John Christopher Willoughby, Fifth Bart., Fulmer Hall, Slough, Buckinghamshire (sold 1906). *Mellon Collection,* 1937. Painted 1781–83.

SIR HENRY RAEBURN (British, 1756–1823)

MISS ELEANOR URQUHART

Catalogue No. 101

Canvas

Height 29⅜″ (75 cm.)
Width 24¼″ (62 cm.)

Flaubert's admonition to artists, 'Be regular and ordinary in your life, like a bourgeois, so that you can be violent and original in your work,' might serve as a description of Sir Henry Raeburn. Art was a business to this most distinguished of Scottish painters, and from nine to five-thirty it kept him regularly in his studio where he painted a succession of three to four sitters a day. When he left his easel, it was to speculate in real estate or to play golf. But conventional as was his life, there was nothing conventional about his portraiture.

As a young man Raeburn decided to record only what he saw in front of him and never to trust his memory even when painting a subordinate part of the picture. This practice, common today, was contrary to the regular procedure of eighteenth-century portraitists. They used instead a pre-established tone for flesh, a traditional arrangement of highlights and shadows, and other fixed conventions. Raeburn, relying on actual observation and not on a memorized formula, developed a style which foreshadows contemporary painting.

For while he anticipates the goal of modern portraitists, seizing in his best works on the salient features of the sitter and rendering them in the moment of conception, his technical performance at times goes beyond the attainments of any contemporary artist. It is amazing that in portraying Miss Urquhart, for example, he did not have to change a single brush stroke. Success in direct painting of this type depends on the swiftness and certainty of the artist's hand. The moment he falters, renders a false shadow, fails to find the correct contour, misses the right color, the passage must be repainted and the freshness is gone.

Raeburn himself failed more often than he succeeded, and his work frequently suffers from the same faults that plague modern portraitists: either the pigment is thick from reworking, or the shadows too black, or the colors dull. *Miss Urquhart* is an exception; and it is easy to imagine that on this occasion, fascinated by the beauty of his sitter, the artist forgot all hesitations and after-thoughts and put down *à premier coup* the image of an aristocratic and charming woman, creating spontaneously one of his supreme masterpieces. Collections: William Urquhart and family, Scotland and Ireland. *Mellon Colletion*, 1937. Painted c. 1795.

BENJAMIN WEST (American, 1738–1820)
COLONEL GUY JOHNSON   Canvas
Catalogue No. 496   Height 79³/₄″ (203 cm.)
                                                     Width 54¹/₂″ (138 cm.)

Though American painting in the eighteenth century was a colonial de-
pendency of British painting, American artists, until they went abroad,
saw very few European pictures. As Copley wrote, 'I think myself pecul-
iarly unlucky in Liveing in a place into which there has not been one portrait brought that is worthy to be call'd a Picture within my memory.'
Under the circumstances it is not surprising that our leading painters should
have found it more congenial to live in England.

Of these expatriates Benjamin West was the first to settle abroad, where
his success was extraordinary. He may well have appeared to Europeans
as a perfect instance of the 'noble savage,' whose interest in art justified the
theories of Jean-Jacques Rousseau. West's biographer, John Galt, relates
that during the artist's visit to Rome in 1760, the Italians, thinking that
he had received the education of a savage, became curious to see the effect
the works of art in the Belvedere and Vatican would have on him. When,
however, he compared the *Apollo Belvedere* to a young Mohawk warrior,
and proceeded to explain the merits of the statue in terms of the analogy
between it and the Mohawk Indians, the Italians were delighted with the
excellence of the criticism and West's popularity was assured. Eventually
he settled in London where he came to be recognized as the foremost
English historical painter. Elected to succeed Sir Joshua Reynolds, he became the second president of the Royal Academy.

West did many large historical canvases for George III and painted
many notable portraits. Of these one of the finest is the portrait of Colonel
Guy Johnson, who was the English Superintendent of Indian Affairs in the
American Colonies. With him West has included an idealized figure of an
Indian holding a peace pipe in contrast with the Englishman's gun. In the
background is an idyllic scene of Indian family life before a huge water-
fall, perhaps Niagara. Possibly the Indian is his famous secretary Joseph
Brant, who was known in his own language as Thayendanegea.

West's treatment of the Indian is so generalized that the face cannot be
identified with known portraits of Brant; it is more probably a 'noble
savage' advocating peace on the eve of the Revolution. Collections: Dina
E. Brown, Henfield, England. *Mellon Collection,* 1940. Painted c. 1775.

GILBERT STUART (American, 1755–1828)
MRS RICHARD YATES   Canvas
Catalogue No. 490   Height 30¼" (77 cm.)
                                                Width 25" (63 cm.)

In two hundred years America has produced several great painters, and among these at least one innovator of genius, Gilbert Stuart. Stuart, who arrived in London in 1775, a penniless young student, owed his training to his compatriot Benjamin West. In West's studio he was taught the accepted methods of eighteenth-century portraiture: a general tint for flesh, certain fixed places for highlights and deep shadows and, often to improve the appearance of the sitter, touches of carmine in the nostrils and the corners of the eyes.

The young American was an apt pupil and soon had 'his full share of the best business in London, and prices equal to any, except Sir Joshua Reynolds and Gainsborough,' to quote a contemporary, Dunlap. But he was not satisfied. As he said, 'I wish to find out what nature is for myself, and see her with my own eyes.'

Such freshness of vision was easier to achieve in the Colonies than in the mother country, for in America no formula for painting had yet been established. Patrons like Mrs Yates, the wife of a New York merchant, wanted to see themselves as they really were, and they were perfectly willing that an artist should make technical experiments if these led to a more accurate portrayal. Thus after his return to America in 1793, Stuart's power of observation increased and he noted, among other facts of vision, that 'Good flesh coloring partook of all colors, not mixed, so as to be combined in one tint, but shining through each other, like the blood through the natural skin.' In following out this and other discoveries about appearance, he broke with the eighteenth-century formula for portraiture and anticipated many of the visual theories of the French Impressionists. Had there been the artists and the tradition of painting in America that there were in France, these innovations of Stuart's might have caused Impressionism to appear in the New World generations before it revolutionized art in Europe. Collections: Carlisle Pollock II, grandson of the sitter, New Orleans; Marie Louise Pollock Chiapella, great-granddaughter of the sitter, New Orleans; Henry Chiapella, great-great-grandson of the sitter, Marguerite Chiapella and Mrs Louise Chiapella Formento, great-great-granddaughters of the sitter, New Orleans; Dr Isaac M. Cline, New Orleans; Thomas B. Clarke, New York. *Mellon Collection*, 1940. Painted in 1793.

JOHN SINGLETON COPLEY (American, 1738–1815)
THE COPLEY FAMILY   Canvas
Catalogue No. 1650   Height 72½" (184.4 cm.)
                                                    Width 90⅜" (229.7 cm.)

John Singleton Copley, the other great American artist of the eighteenth
century, while painting in his native Boston, was just as unflattering as
Stuart in his portrayals. He did not, however, remain in New England for
long.

His wife's father, Richard Clarke, was a consignee of the famous shipment of tea from England that was sent contrary to the wishes of the
Colonists, only to be thrown into the harbor in the Boston Tea Party.
Consequently this Tory merchant left the Colonies in high dudgeon and
in low repute. Copley, who had been studying abroad, soon after joined
his father-in-law in London, where he remained the rest of his life. Shortly
after his arrival he painted the group portrait which we reproduce.

Mrs Copley and her father sit in the foreground, surrounded by the little
Copleys, while the artist looks out pensively from behind and clutches all
that remained of his New England prosperity—a few sheets of drawings.
Copley had reached a crossroads in his life. He was settled in England,
faced with the necessity of making his way in an alien country where
standards were very different from those he had left behind in Boston. He
decided to change his whole approach to portraiture. *The Copley Family*
shows, side by side, his old and his new style. The painting of his father-
in-law, especially his hands, and the charmingly-rendered doll in the corner
of the picture, are the last echoes of that visual truth which characterized
his early work. The painting of his wife, of the children, the composition
of the picture, all are reminiscent of Reynolds, of West, of the 'grand
manner' of portraiture, which Copley forced himself to adopt. He was
successful for a period, being elected a member of the Royal Academy, but
he fell out of fashion. And though he painted more industriously than ever,
he was unable to gain back his reputation. The end of his life was sad, for
he was constantly menaced by debts and seems to have been sensitive that
he had betrayed his original gifts. Collections: Copley family, London and
Boston. *National Gallery of Art Purchase Fund, Andrew W. Mellon Gift,*
1961. Painted 1776.

GOYA (Spanish, 1746–1828)   Canvas
MARQUESA DE PONTEJOS
Catalogue No. 85   Height 83" (211 cm.) Width 49³/₄" (126 cm.)

The last of Spain's great painters, Goya was influenced, as were the
American Colonial artists, by British painting. True, he knew the works
of Gainsborough and Reynolds only in mezzotint engravings, but from
prints after their portraits he learned to convey an impression of elegance
and luxury. However, as a society portraitist in the English sense, his
character was flawed. He could not take his sitters seriously. The Marquesa
is just a little ridiculous. She is a fashion plate, as much the product of
artificial selection as her pug dog. Her tulle skirt was more amusing to Goya
than her insipid face. It offered him an opportunity to paint her portrait
in a mockingly-light palette with piquant alternations of sweet and acid
colors.   *Continued on page 215*

GOYA (Spanish, 1746–1828)   Canvas
DOÑA TERESA SUREDA
Catalogue No. 549   Height 47¹/₈" (119.8 cm.) Width 31¹/₄" (79.4 cm.)

Sometimes a painting is more interesting when considered in conjunction
with its pendant. To appreciate fully the portrait of Doña Teresa, look on
page 281 where a portrait by Goya of her husband is reproduced. He was
a painter, one of the first Spanish lithographers, an authority on the manu-
facture of glass, porcelain, and textiles and, from 1804 to 1808, the director
of the royal porcelain factory of the Buen Retiro in Madrid, where he
introduced the production of Sèvres porcelain. He was also Goya's friend,
and they must in all probability have spent many late and companionable
evenings together. On their return one can easily imagine that they were
confronted by this icy, outraged woman. Goya has painted not only a
portrait but a point of view – the intolerance of uncompromising rectitude.
Note the stiff line of Doña Teresa's back and how her resentment is conveyed by her hard, staring eyes and her sullen mouth. Here is a whole novel
in two pictures.

Goya's portraits are different from those of earlier artists. Velázquez, for
example, portrays his sitters with complete detachment, imposing no mood
whatever, permitting us to make our own judgment; Rembrandt sees his
subject as an opportunity to convey his own tragic feelings; Frans Hals
presents his men and women with a photographic superficiality which
Continued on page 220

WILLIAM BLAKE (British, 1757–1827)
THE GREAT RED DRAGON AND THE WOMAN
CLOTHED WITH THE Sun   Watercolor
Catalogue No. B-11,064   Height 15³/₄″ (40 cm.)
                                                 Width 12³/₄″ (32.5 cm.)

This is the only watercolor reproduced in this book. But it is not only the
technique which is different. William Blake's style is in complete contrast
to the work of the other artists. The greatest poet-painter in history, with
the possible exception of Michelangelo, this strange, impassioned being was
considered by many of his contemporaries to be mad. Yet he remains the
noblest astronaut of the mind in art or literature. His imaginative explora-
tion of the far reaches of the immaterial, as in the work reproduced, has
provided us with awe-inspiring data of the cosmic tempests and the serene
beauty of the world of the spirit.

Although Blake does not follow the exact details, his watercolor is an
illustration of Revelation 12: 'And there appeared a great wonder in
heaven; a woman clothed with the sun, and the moon under her feet, and
upon her head a crown of twelve stars ... And there appeared another
wonder in heaven; and behold a great red dragon, having seven heads and
ten horns, and seven crowns upon his heads.'

The Great Red Dragon, the incarnation of Satanic evil, seeks to devour
the still unborn child of the Woman Clothed with the Sun, symbol of
valiant innocence.

The watercolor belonged originally to Thomas Butts who purchased
drawings from Blake, sometimes at the rate of one a week, until his house
was filled with these strange and wonderful pictures. It was his friendship
and patronage which enabled Blake to produce a steady stream of original
work. That Blake should have had to depend to this extent on a single
patron, and that his work should have been so little understood by his
contemporaries, is an indication of a profound change in the role of art in
society. Collections: Thomas Butts, London; A. Edward Newton, Philadelphia. *Rosenwald Collection,* 1943. Signed with initials. Painted probably
between 1805 and 1810, when Blake painted most of his watercolors.

JOHN CONSTABLE (British, 1776–1837)   Canvas
WIVENHOE PARK, ESSEX
Catalogue No. 606   Height 22¹/₈″ (56.1 cm.) Width 39⁷/₈″ (101.2 cm.)

'Arcadian realism' may seem a contradictory term, but it describes the charm of many of Constable's canvases. His scenes are filled with poetry, visions of the tranquil delight of an ideal rural existence. Yet, at the same time, they have an extraordinary reality, conveying as they do flashes of insight into the momentary moods of nature with that sensibility which is at the heart of modern landscape painting.

The wish of the owner to see as much as possible of his estate explains the unusually wide angle of the artist's view. But Constable, by the actuality he gives *Wivenhoe Park*, triumphs over this difficult composition and makes us agree with General Rebow that it would not be possible to see too much of so entrancing a scene. So there is no necessity for the twilight with which earlier landscapists gave a romantic aspect to their Arcadian scenery. Instead, Constable has found in a typical English day of scattered clouds and brilliant sunshine a new inspiration. Painting was changed by such a fresh observation of landscape, just as poetry was changed at about the same time by Wordsworth's descriptions of nature. Collections: Wivenhoe Park, Essex. *Widener Collection*, 1942. Painted 1816.

JOSEPH MALLORD WILLIAM TURNER (British, 1775–1851) Canvas
MORTLAKE TERRACE
Catalogue No. 109   Height 35³/₄″ (90 cm.) Width 47¹/₂″ (95 cm.)

In 1827 Turner exhibited at the Royal Academy the picture reproduced, which was entitled *Mortlake Terrace, the Seat of William Moffatt, Esq.; Summer's Evening.* The preceding year he had exhibited the same site seen from the opposite direction and bathed in the light of an early summer morning, a picture now in the Frick Collection in New York. These two canvases were executed at a moment of significant change in Turner's style: a period when light and the rendering of a visible atmosphere were becoming his preoccupation, to the exclusion of his earlier interest in topography. Though he was doubtless fulfilling a commission in depicting Mr Moffatt's garden terrace from opposite points and under contrasting illumination, Turner's whole effort was concentrated on the atmospheric envelope of the scene, on rendering the sun-filled mist of a hot afternoon. Collections: Joseph Hamatt; Rev. Edward J. Daniel; Thomas Creswick, R.A.; E. B. Fripp; Samuel Ashton; Thomas Ashton; Mrs Elizabeth Gair Ashton. *Mellon Collection.* Painted c. 1826.

JACQUES-LOUIS DAVID (French, 1748–1825)
NAPOLEON IN HIS STUDY   Canvas
Catalogue No. 1374   Height 80¼" (203.9 cm.)
                                                 Width 49¼" (125.1 cm.)

How much our concept of historic personages depends upon the artists who portrayed them! Compared to Napoleon, men like Doge Gritti (page 136) or Giuliano de' Medici (page 85) were insignificant. Yet no one who painted the Emperor was able to give him an appearance of authority, of human grandeur. Perhaps Napoleon lived too late. The available artists were incapable of creating an image commensurate with his achievement. David tried, but has managed merely to supply a mass of external trappings.

The Emperor's uniform combines details of the Grenadiers of his famous Imperial Guard with the epaulettes of a general. He wears the insignia of the Legion of Honor, which he created. Beneath the table is a copy of Plutarch's *Lives*. The manuscript of the *Code Napoléon* is on the desk. The pen and scattered papers, the candles burning to their sockets, and the clock pointing to quarter-past four, all indicate that the Emperor has just finished a hard night's work. This unmitigated flattery caused the Emperor to say to the artist. 'You have understood me, David. By night I work for the welfare of my subjects, and by day for their glory.'

Just as the portrait of Gritti probably held a special significance for Charles I, so this portrait of Napoleon, a masterpiece of political propaganda, must have had its own meaning for another Briton, the Duke of Hamilton. This eccentric peer believed himself to be the rightful heir to the throne of Scotland. He wished to have in his house full-length portraits of the rulers of Europe and, though Napoleon had been for years the archenemy of his country, the Duke had no hesitation in commissioning David to paint the Emperor.

The portrait is dated 1812, the year the Imperial armies were freezing during the retreat from Moscow, but it is believed to have been ordered in 1810, when English troops were fighting Napoleon in Portugal. Collections: Marquess of Douglas (Alexander, tenth Duke of Hamilton), Hamilton Palace, near Glasgow; Earl of Rosebery, London. *Samuel H. Kress Collection*, 1954. Signed, and dated 1812.

JEAN-AUGUSTE-DOMINIQUE INGRES (French, 1780–1867)

MADAME MOITESSIER   Canvas

Catalogue No. 882   Height 58¹/₄″ (148 cm.)

Width 40″ (101.6 cm.)

Fashion in feminine beauty is as variable as fashions in clothes. Occasionally this mutability of taste affects the appreciation of a work of art. Many people today, for example, would consider Madame Moitessier, as she appears in her portrait by Ingres, an ugly woman, corpulent and bovine.

Yet to Ingres, the outstanding master of the French academic school, she was the reincarnation of a goddess of the ancient world, an archetype of the beautiful woman.

Ingres in many of his letters extolled his model's appearance, but he seems to have had only a secondary interest in her personality. He worked for months on her portrait, finishing the dress and accessories; then he added the arms and hands; and finally he attached the head to the bare shoulders. Painting backwards, so to speak, he treated his picture less as portraiture than as still life, and concentrated his immense virtuosity on painting Madame Moitessier's clothes, jewels, fan, and beside her the chair with gloves and fur jacket. It is Ingres' marvelous conjunction of eye and hand apparent in such passages, the way he renders the subtle ellipses of flesh in the fat arms, the depth of translucence in the rubies and sapphires, the sheen of the pearl necklace, the subtle distinction between the gilt of the chair and the gold of the bracelets, that shows his mastery of realistic detail. Collections: Comtesse de Flavigny (née Moitessier); Vicomtesse O. de Bondy, (née Moitessier); Comte Olivien de Bondy, Château de la Barre (Indre). *Samuel H. Kress Collection*, 1945. Signed, and dated 1851.

Continued from page 207

In this work of Goya's early years there appears for the first time a note that is sardonic, even cynical. This was to swell to the terrifying chord, the clash of horror, the rumble of social systems in collapse that is heard with such fearful force in the great masterpieces of Goya's later years. This combination of a much deeper seriousness and a bitter disbelief in all established things provided a basis for those revolutions in painting which, under his influence, took place in France in the next century. Goya's *Marquesa* marks the beginning of a turning point in art. Collections: Marquesa de Martorell y de Pontejos, Madrid; Marqués de Miraflores y de Pontejos, Madrid. *Mellon Collection*, 1937. Painted possibly 1786.

JEAN-BAPTISTE-CAMILLE COROT (French, 1796—1875)

AGOSTINA Canvas

Catalogue No. D-13 Height 52¼" (132.8 cm.)

Width 37⅜" (95 cm.)

Time may prove Corot to have been the most important painter of the nineteenth century. Certainly the admiration he has aroused in other artists has been unceasing, and his influence even on contemporary painters like Picasso, immense. He was one of the few artists of recent times to excel not only in landscape, but also in figure painting, of which *Agostina* is an outstanding example. Here he combines an alertness of vision with a profound knowledge of Renaissance style. This Italian peasant girl, who stands with unself-conscious detachment, evokes the heroic women of Piero della Francesca. But she is also of her own century, for she has been observed by the artist with an enamored and penetrating scrutiny which brings her much closer to actuality, to the living model, than her fifteenth-century forebears.

The plastic values which distinguish Corot's best landscapes are due in part to his constant study of human form. This is of importance in understanding his work. There is a profound difference in style between those landscape painters who are either incapable of drawing the human form or draw it in a perfunctory way, and those whose art is based on a knowledge of the body. In one category we have artists like Perugino, Claude Lorrain, most of the Dutch landscape painters with the significant exception of Rembrandt, and in the nineteenth century, Monet. All of these artists could draw the human figure after a fashion, but none of them was a figure painter of any consequence. In their landscapes we find that such effects as the sweep of distance and the play of light are stressed, but in the beautiful iridescent spaces they create, everything is insubstantial, intangible. The other category, those artists like Corot, who have mastered the hollows and bosses of the human form, its plastic shape, seem able to translate this knowledge of mass and volume into hills and rocks and trees. Painters like Rubens, Poussin, Rembrandt, Cézanne and, at his best, Corot, are intent on rendering the plastic character of nature. They model trees and rocks with the same studious gravity they show toward the human body. They seem to be in search of the tendons and sinews of nature. Collections: Breysse, Paris; Faure, Paris; Paton, Paris; Bernheim-Jeune, Paris. *Chester Dale Collection*, 1941. Signed. Painted probably 1866.

216

JEAN-BAPTISTE-CAMILLE COROT (French, 1796–1875)
A VIEW NEAR VOLTERRA   Canvas
Catalogue No. D-14   Height 27³/₈″ (69.5 cm.)
                                             Width 37¹/₂″ (95.2 cm.)

A View near Volterra belongs to Corot's earlier style. It is dated 1838, four
years after he had visited the Etruscan site of Volterra. It is therefore a
souvenir d'Italie, an evocation of a mood the artist had felt when he
entered that strange, wild country, that *pays magnifique*, as he described
it in his sketchbook. But the painting itself was based on careful studies
and sketches made at the time, and it seems to fulfill the profession of a
faith which Corot expressed in his youth when he wrote, *'Il ne faut laisser
d'indécision dans aucune chose.'* Consequently, we feel in the scene itself
the same sense of a vivid reality which the artist experienced as he sketched
one day in the early summer sunlight, yet we also feel that the emotion
conveyed is an 'emotion recollected in tranquility,' a mood revived long
after the event by some nostalgia, some longing for the olive greens and
soft, luminous skies of Italy. This has given to the painting qualities both
of timelessness and of actuality, qualities which Corot himself seems to have
appreciated; for we find that he often returned in this way to scenes he had
enjoyed on his early Italian journeys. Led by these recollections he painted
from memory again and again the sights of classical civilization, the world
of Horace and Vergil, whose feelings for nature were so akin to his own.
   It is curious, however, how little these superb paintings of Italy were
appreciated during Corot's lifetime. The opinions of the critics on *A View
near Volterra*, which was probably first exhibited at the Salon of 1838,
are typical. They found it cold, timid in execution, without distinction or
brilliance. They failed to see its real importance: that it was a remarkable
revival of the classical tradition, and that it illustrated what Cézanne had
in mind when he is quoted as saying, *'Imaginez Poussin refait entièrement
sur nature.'* For Corot's landscapes of this period possess the formal beauty
of Poussin's style without his artificiality, his declamatory effects, his suggestion of stage scenery. It was the blindness of the critics, year after year,
which caused Corot to compromise and to give the classical style a sentimental interpretation. But as the familiar gray mist spread through his
landscapes, his extraordinary gift for the rendering of plastic volume disappeared. Collections: Baronne Thénard, Paris. *Chester Dale Collection,*
1941. Signed, and dated 1838.

HONORÉ DAUMIER (French, 1808–1879)
ADVICE TO A YOUNG ARTIST   Canvas
Catalogue No. 545   Height 16⅛″ (41 cm.)
                                                   Width 12⅞″ (33 cm.)

Corot's figure style influenced the work of his close companion, Daumier. The two artists had much in common–both sought and found the true tradition of painting in the Italian masters. Balzac said of Daumier, 'He is a man who has something of Michelangelo in his blood.' But this great talent had to be lavished on caricatures for various periodicals. Poverty left Daumier little time for painting, and with failing eyesight he could not draw and sell his famous cartoons fast enough to pay his rent, even for the dilapidated cottage he occupied at Valmondois. But he was fortunate in one thing–in friendship. Corot secretly bought Daumier's house, and wrote him as follows: 'My old comrade,–I had a little house for which I had no use at Valmondois near the Isle-Adam. The idea came into my head of offering it to you, and as I think it is a good idea, I have placed it in your name at the notary's. It is not for you that I do this, it is merely to annoy your landlord.' It was a simple gesture, and it gave Daumier a few serene and tranquil years. But it meant that Corot painted fewer Agostinas and more misty lakes, fewer masterpieces and more potboilers. In return for this sacrifice, a few paintings like this, which once belonged to Corot, were all that Daumier could give his old friend, but into their execution he poured all the brilliant genius that a lifetime of poverty could not destroy. Collections: J.-B.-C. Corot, Paris; Adolphe A. Tavernier, Paris; Cronier, Paris; Georg, Rheims. *Gift of Duncan Phillipps,* 1941. Painted probably after 1860.

Continued from page 207

makes them seem acquaintances who will never become friends. Goya, on the other hand, analyzes character in relation to social position and environment. Occasionally one seems even to sense the sitter's reaction to a particular situation. This type of analysis, a combination of sociology and psychology, was a distinct innovation in portraiture and a remarkable contribution to art. Collections: The family of the sitter; Havemeyer, New York. *Gift of Mr and Mrs P. H. B. Frelinghuysen in memory of her father and mother, Mr and Mrs H. O. Havemeyer,* 1941. Painted c.1805.

220

CHARLES-FRANÇOIS DAUBIGNY (French, 1817–1878)   Canvas
THE FARM   Height 20½" (52.1 cm.)
Catalogue No. D-18   Width 31¾" (80.6 cm.)

Sketching the river life and countryside of central France, as he drifted
down the Oise in the curious floating studio he had built himself, Daubigny
appeared to the Impressionists as an accepted master come to justify their
methods of painting, their out-of-doors studies made directly from nature.
And yet *The Farm*, dated 1855, with its sensitive feeling for sequence and
interval, with its skillfully balanced masses and its elimination of all un-
essential detail, with its simplification of the pictorial problem to a few
significant elements – three houses silhouetted against the sky and a wall
and a cart – goes beyond Impressionism to become a forerunner of the art
of our time. But the solidity of structure and pure, almost stark design so
conspicuous in *The Farm* appear in only one or two early landscapes by
Daubigny. Most of his work shows a more poetic and intimate, though less
organized, interpretation of nature. Thus, he remained essentially the prophet of Impressionism and left to a later genius, Cézanne, the role of precursor of modern painting. Collections: Gérard, Paris. *Chester Dale Collection,* 1941. Signed, and dated 1855.

EDOUARD MANET (French, 1832–1883)   Canvas
THE OLD MUSICIAN   Height 73¾" (187.5 cm.)
Catalogue No. D-25   Width 98" (249.1 cm.)

The principal pleasure to be gained from Manet comes from the beauty of
his brushwork. He mixed on his palette the exact tone he needed and with
swift and certain dexterity delineated on the canvas each area of light and
shadow. In *The Old Musician* this virtuosity of handling can be seen most
clearly in the trenchant strokes that define the folds in the shirt and trousers
of the boy with the straw hat, or in the more caressing feather touch on
the shawl of the girl holding the baby.

Manet's method of direct painting caused him to suppress the transitional
tones of modeling which particularly suggest volume. Like Velázquez, who
was also a master of brushwork, he chose an illumination which would
flatten form as much as possible. Thus the light falls directly on the figures
from behind the artist's head, and the shadows are reduced to a minimum.
Through this arbitrary elimination of shadow Manet was able to state local
color more freely. He attained, especially in such early works as *The Old*
Continued on page 224

EDOUARD MANET (French, 1832–1883)

GARE ST-LAZARE   Canvas
Catalogue No. 1454   Height 36³/₄″ (93.3 cm.)
                                                Width 45¹/₈″ (114.5 cm.)

Why does this painting convey such a sense of gaiety? There is, of course,
the marvelous observation of the little sleeping dog, one of the most enchanting puppies in art. There is also the pretty Victorine Meurend, whose
beauty is more familiar to us from pictures ten years earlier, *Olympia* and
Le Déjeuner sur L'herbe. Dressed or undressed she is a joy, delighting us
with the wonderfully candid gaze of a woman to whom shyness is unknown.
But the real source of our pleasure, the heroine of the picture, is the little
girl, the daughter of Manet's friend Alphonse Hirsch. From the way she
holds the railing, from the angle of her head, from the beautiful line made
by the curve of her neck, we know the intensity of her scrutiny. We share
the excitement we felt in childhood at seeing trains, and steam, and smoke.
Manet knew better than anyone else how to catch the fugitive charm of
everyday life. He was a master of the informal composition. He had a keen
sense of the immediacy this type of design can convey. The *Gare St-Lazare*
is a family snapshot. But this moment of time, made timeless, is held with
a beauty and intensity far beyond the possibilities of photography.

The painting was admitted, somewhat unexpectedly, to the Salon of 1874,
where it aroused more protests than praise. It was the first large canvas
Manet had executed mostly out-of-doors, perhaps acknowledging thereby
his association with the younger Impressionists, Monet and Renoir especially,
who had for some time been working in the open air. Thus it carried into
the citadel of the official Salon the banner of their revolt. Collections:
Jean-Baptiste Faure, Paris; Durand-Ruel, New York; Havemeyer family,
New York. *Gift of Horace Havemeyer in memory of his mother Louisine
W. Havemeyer*, 1956. Signed, and dated 1873.

Continued from page 223
Musician, the most subtle harmonies of yellowish white and faded blue,
here contrasted with warm browns and blacks and soft grays. This color
scheme was as far as possible from the high intensities and broken colors of
the Impressionists, which he adopted at the end of his life.
Collections: Manet family, Paris; Prince de Wagram, Paris; P.R.Pearson,
Paris; Imperial Museum, Vienna; C.C.Hodeberg, Paris. *Chester Dale
Collection*, 1941. Signed, and dated 1862.

BERTHE MORISOT (French, 1841–1895)

THE MOTHER AND SISTER OF THE ARTIST

Canvas

Catalogue No. D-26

Height 39³/₄″ (101 cm.)
Width 32¹/₄″ (82 cm.)

The question is constantly asked, 'How should my son (or daughter) learn to be a painter?' When Madame Morisot put this question to Guichard about her daughter, Berthe, then aged fifteen, the painter answered, 'The first thing to do, Madame, is to get your daughter permission to work in the Louvre, where I shall give my instruction in front of the masters.' The answer was not surprising, for the Louvre was the traditional art school of all French painters of ability. There, as Ingres said, they sought to draw out from the Old Masters, *'le suc de la plante,'* that quintessential quality which is in all *great* art. This intelligent use of the Louvre explains to a large extent the superiority of French painting in the last century. Berthe Morisot was an assiduous copyist. She began with the Old Masters and ended with Corot, whose work she had the advantage of discussing with the artist himself. In the Louvre she often saw Manet, the brother of her future husband. During the winter before the outbreak of the Franco-Prussian War, when she was just twenty-nine, she completed the portrait of her mother and sister and asked Manet to come to her studio to give her a criticism. He was delighted with the picture, but suggested a few changes and then seized the brush and spent the afternoon retouching it. His brush strokes are still visible in the somewhat heavier touch around the eye and mouth of Madame Morisot and the thicker impasto of her dress. While Manet was working, the van to take the picture to the Salon arrived, and Berthe Morisot, though she was angry, could do nothing but send the painting as it was. Fortunately, the canvas was received with enthusiasm by many artists, especially by Fantin-Latour, and the painter herself became reconciled to the changes. Collections: Pontillon family, Paris. *Chester Dale Collection*, 1941. Painted during the winter of 1869–70.

AUGUSTE RENOIR (French, 1841–1919)
A Girl with a Watering Can   Canvas
Catalogue No. D-31   Height 39¹/₂" (100 cm.)
                                                 Width 28³/₄" (73 cm.)

A Girl with a Watering Can, painted in 1876, is one of the most popular
pictures in the National Gallery. It is evocative of sunlight and childhood,
springtime and the breath of flowers, images and sensations which are in
themselves attractive. But these are not enough. To be great a painting
must have more than charm of subject matter; it must have certain aesthetic
values as well. In the case of *A Girl with a Watering Can* these values
consist largely in the relationship of figure and landscape, in the way the
two are fused by ingenious repetition of colors and a consistent treatment
of detail. The whole picture is made up of a web of brilliantly colored
brush strokes, which from a distance are seen to be a child, roses, grass,
a garden path. The little girl seems to merge with her surroundings, to
become one with the variegated tones of nature. This creates a mysterious
sense of interrelations, as though one substance permeated humanity, vegeta-
tion, and earth.

The unity of figure and background Renoir extends to a psychological
unity between himself and the child. The scene is depicted from the level
of the little girl's own vision, so that her outlook on nature is suggested.
Thus the garden becomes the world seen through her eyes, narrow and
circumscribed. By accepting her scale of observation, Renoir evokes, in an
almost unique way, memories of childhood. This mood, this 'remembrance
of things past,' is intensified by the pleasure of the painter in his subject,
by the spontaneity and gaiety of his treatment of the scene. Renoir, in
canvases like this, seems almost a pagan Fra Angelico. 'I arrange my subject
as I want it,' he once said, 'and then I go ahead and paint it like a child.'
He loved bright colors, joyous and pretty human beings, and nature
drenched in sunshine. Collections: Paul Bérard, Paris; A. Rosenberg, Paris;
Prince de Wagram, Paris. *Chester Dale Collection,* 1941. Signed, and dated
1876.

228

EDGAR DEGAS (French, 1834–1917)
MADAME RENÉ DE GAS   Canvas
Catalogue No. D-20   Height 28⁵/₈″ (72.7 cm.)
                                            Width 36¹/₄″ (92 cm.)

With tactful subtlety Degas has suggested the blind, unfocused stare of
his sister-in-law. The portrait seems unposed, the sitter unself-conscious.
Thus Degas conveys that feeling of fortuitous objectivity which was his
goal in portraiture. As he once said, he was interested in doing 'portraits
of people in familiar and typical attitudes, above all in giving to their
faces the same choice of expression as one gives to their bodies.' Consequently, he sought to transcribe appearance accurately, to achieve photographic veracity, as though the camera had just clicked and the artist had
transposed to the canvas his exact mental picture. But though the casual
yet perfectly balanced design of this picture has the immediacy of a snapshot, the artist, because draftsmanship is more flexible than photography,
has been able to eliminate all extraneous detail and to concentrate attention
on the important features of his sitter. Unfortunately, contemporary portraiture has lost the secret of combining aesthetic perception with photographic likeness. Collections: Degas Sale, 1918; Henry D. Hughes, New
York. *Chester Dale Collection,* 1941. Painted in the winter of 1872–73.

EDGAR DEGAS (French, 1834–1917)
FOUR DANCERS   Canvas
Catalogue No. D-22   Height 59¹/₄″ (50.5 cm.)
                                            Width 71¹/₄″ (181 cm.)

Degas found a rich mine of casual yet perfectly balanced arrangements
in the ballet, as one can see in the picture reproduced. There is no question
that he was helped to discover these ready-made compositions by Japanese
prints. The Japanese printmakers sought to make their woodcuts a mirror
of the passing world, and Impressionism had essentially the same goal. But
the Impressionists, especially Degas, went far deeper into the study of
appearance than the superficial actuality of Japanese prints. In a way that
would have been inconceivable for Eastern artists, these French painters
were scientists, intent upon analysis of vision. In his painting of *Four
Dancers* Degas is experimenting with effects of artificial illumination, with
the appearance of these ballet dancers under beams of green and red spot-
lights. Collections: Degas' atelier until 1918; Wilhelm Hansen, Copenhagen.
Chester Dale Collection, 1941. Atelier stamp: Degas. Painted about 1899.

CLAUDE MONET (French, 1840–1926)

Palazzo da Mula, Venice   Canvas

Catalogue No. D-64   Height 24^1/$_2$" (62.2 cm.)

Width 32" (81.3 cm.)

In Venice substance often seems to dissolve into reflection while light appears as material and palpable as the object it falls on. Then churches, palaces, and bridges are transmuted into curtains of colored light, wavering and trembling in their aqueous mirror; and nature, transformed by this amphibious atmosphere, becomes the imitator of art, creating scenery as insubstantially evanescent as the most Impressionistic painting. No wonder that Claude Monet, when he finally reached Venice in 1908, wrote to Gustave Geffroy, 'all this unusual light. ... It is so beautiful! ... However, I am having a delicious time here and can almost forget that once I was not the old man I am now!'

But looking at the *Palazzo da Mula* the question arises: has Monet gone too far in his interpretation of this light? At twilight did he actually see Venice as an architecture of amethysts, turquoise, emeralds, and rubies? Or is such a vision of intense color only a poetic invention and the reality much less colorful, much closer to the gray and black the average person sees? The answer is complicated and goes to the heart of the problem of Impressionism. What we see in the field of vision are relationships of areas of color and of light and shadow. These relationships the Impressionist painter wished to express, but he was hampered by the limitations of pigment. In the present scene, for instance, no oil paint could give the luminosity of the darkening water nor the blackness of the velvety shadows as they actually appeared. Therefore many of the Impressionists, and Monet especially, decided to compensate for the deficiencies of paint, its narrower range of contrasting values, by using contrasting colors of an intensity greater than those they observed in the scene they were painting. From this point of view the *Palazzo da Mula* is true to nature's organization of tones; but it is a transposition into another key, one with a more limited scale of light and shadow but, as compensation, with a greater brilliance of color. Thus, though Monet never saw a building like this, a palace made of a rubble of precious stones, his canvas is still a close approximation to the relationship of light, shadow, and color in nature. Collections: Arthur B. Emmons, Newport, Rhode Island; Henry D. Hughes, New York. *Chester Dale Collection*, 1942. Signed, and dated 1908.

HENRI FANTIN-LATOUR (French, 1836–1904)   Canvas
STILL LIFE
Catalogue No. D-24   Height 24³/₈″ (61.9 cm.) Width 29¹/₂″ (75 cm.)

Many people do not understand why artists take such pleasure in still-life painting. For example, in the picture reproduced, what was it that really interested Fantin-Latour? Obviously the rendering of actual appearance. But how is that done? The answer lies in the organization of detail, tone, and texture. Detail involves distance and time of vision. Should the artist paint what he would see when closely scrutinizing his subject through a magnifying glass, or when glancing at it quickly from a greater distance with half-closed eyes, or when looking at it repeatedly from a normal distance? The first method leads to those canvases in which a fly invariably crawls across a leaf or petal toward a drop of water, and the second to the broad abstract patterns which Cézanne has handed on to modern painting. Fantin-Latour, however, chooses the third and represents the amount of detail, the petals of the camelias, the skin of the fruit, the wicker of the basket discernible by normal sight at the distance from which the picture is painted.
Collections: Reginald Davis, Paris; A. T. Hollingsworth, London. *Chester Dale Collection,* 1941. Signed, and dated 1866.

PAUL CÉZANNE (French, 1839–1906)   Canvas
STILL LIFE
Catalogue No. D-11   Height 25⁷/₈″ (65.5 cm.) Width 32¹/₄″ (82 cm.)

The points made in the preceding note will be clearer if one compares the still life reproduced here with the still life by Fantin-Latour (page 235). In the painting by Fantin-Latour the texture, tone, and color of the camelias, the fruit, the china, and the blue book are so skillfully organized that merely visual facts take on a quality of poetry. This is Impressionism insofar as the main interest on the part of the artist is in transcribing a visual impression as accurately as possible, using the highest key of color which can be consistently maintained. But it is also more traditional than the work of the Impressionists, closer to eighteenth-century painters like Chardin, who observe their subject with a steady gaze instead of a quick glance used by Impressionist artists. On the other hand, the still-life painting by Cézanne belongs to a different tradition. It is as far from Impressionism as it is from Chardin. It recalls instead the designs of the

Continued on page 239

PAUL CÉZANNE (French, 1839–1906)
HOUSE OF PÈRE LACROIX
Catalogue No. D-45

Canvas
Height 24¹/₄" (61.5 cm.)
Width 20" (51 cm.)

Paul Cézanne's life was consecrated to painting. In his lonely retreat at Aix he once wrote to Emile Bernard, 'I have sworn to die painting'; and he carried out his vow, for he was found after a torrential downpour of rain, unconscious beside his easel. A passer-by carried him home in a laundry cart; yet the next morning he struggled back to his studio, was again stricken and died a few days later.

What was the vision he followed with such passion and such relentlessness? As nearly as words can describe such matters, his quest was twofold: to discover a means of transcribing the weft of color that in nature covers and yet indicates mass, and to find a way of conveying an impression of space without destroying these color relations. In the present landscape, for example, which he painted at Auvers, near Paris, in 1873, he wished to show the trees and the walls of the cottages not only as the colored patterns of light and shade which would have satisfied an Impressionist painter, but also to communicate his perception of their volumes, the dense mass of the foliage and the solidity of the buildings. Similarly, he wished to transcend Impressionism in the rendering of space. Instead of allowing the colors to fade into a misty background, the conventional method of suggesting recession, he wanted to maintain chromatic intensity even in the distance. Thus local color in the *House of Père Lacroix* retains its strength in every plane; and space is created not by diminution of tonal contrast, but by the position and the scale of the trees, the cottages, and the hill, which make up the scene. The magic of Cézanne's style consists in his power to suggest, through selection of color and organization of form, solid volumes in a sequence of planes, aspects of vision which we experience more intensely in his paintings than we do when we look directly at nature. Collections: Alphonse Kann, St Germain-en-Laye, France; Auguste Pellerin, Paris. *Chester Dale Collection*, 1942. Signed, and dated 1873, and exhibited in the Salon of 1873.

236

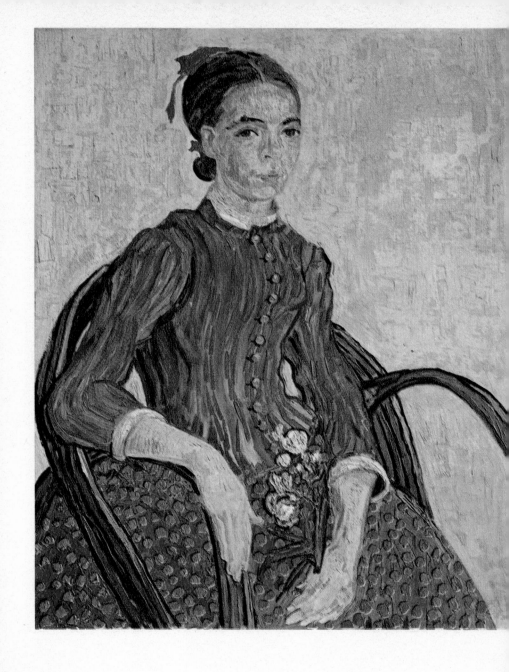

VINCENT VAN GOGH (Dutch, 1853–1890) Canvas
LA MOUSMÉ
Catalogue No. D-76 Height 28⁷/₈" (73.4 cm.) Width 23³/₄" (60 cm.)

Cézanne was not the only artist to react against Impressionism, against its absorption in the fact of vision. Van Gogh also wished to escape the Impressionist tyranny of the eye, to go beyond the mere transcriptions of appearance. A study of Japanese prints liberated him. From them he learned to paint in masses of flat tone or masses of but slightly broken color, and to treat the picture surface as decoration.

Van Gogh wrote his brother, 'I envy the Japanese the extreme clearness which everything has in their work. It is never tedious, and never seems to be done too hurriedly. Their work is as simple as breathing, and they do a figure in a few sure strokes with the same ease as if it were as simple as buttoning your coat.' But van Gogh never attained this facility. He wrote again in July 1888 of *La Mousmé*, 'It took me a whole week, I have not been able to do anything else, not having been very well either ... but I had to reserve my mental energy to do the *mousmé* well. A *mousmé* is a Japanese girl – Provençal in this case – 12 to 14 years old.' Creation was easier for the Japanese artist. He was a member of a group, where everyone worked in the same tradition, but van Gogh was a lonely individual, never sure of his way, only certain that he must follow his self-destroying search for beauty. Collections: Mme J. van Gogh-Bonger, Amsterdam; Carl Sternheim, La Hulpe, Belgium; Alphonse Kann, St Germain-en-Laye, France; J. B. Stang, Oslo. *Chester Dale Collection*, 1942. Painted 1888.

Continued from page 235
great Italian artists, for it has the same gravity and momentum of rhythm we find in the figure paintings of Giotto and Masaccio. The various objects which in Fantin-Latour's still life remain isolated, are here united by continuous movement suggested by the pattern in the folds of the cloth and the napkin, a movement controlled and checked by the emphasized rectangular lines in the background. In Cézanne one finds again the permanent equilibrium characteristic of classical design. Cézanne is not dependent on visual memory for his composition; for he had instead an extraordinary gift of visual imagination, of that genius for inventing compositions which we find in the major Renaissance artists. Collections: Ambroise Vollard, Paris; Maurice Gangnat, Paris; Emil Staub, Switzerland. *Chester Dale Collection*, 1941. Painted about 1890.

PAUL GAUGUIN (French, 1848—1903)
FATATA TE MITI   Canvas
Catalogue No. D-55   Height 26³/₄″ (68 cm.)
                                                 Width 36″ (91.5 cm.)

Paul Gauguin, when already a man of middle age, abandoned his pros-
perous brokerage business, his wife and children, and ultimately all
civilized life to devote himself to painting. Some daemon of creativity
drove him toward an exotic world, first to Panama, where he worked as
a digger on the canal, then to Martinique, where the climate nearly killed
him, and finally, after seventeen months of poverty in France, to the
tropics again, first to Tahiti and later to the Marquesas and a solitary
death at La Dominique.

The present picture, dated 1892, was painted a few months after Gauguin's first arrival at Tahiti. Disgusted with the European character of
life at Papeete, he had withdrawn to the interior of the island to live
among the natives. Tehura, a Polynesian of great beauty, became his *vahine*
and probably posed for the figure of the girl on the right removing her
sarong.

It was during these brief halcyon days that Gauguin developed his
theories of the analogy of color to music. 'Are not these repetitions of
tone,' he was later to ask, 'these monotonous color harmonies (in the
musical sense) analogous to Oriental chants sung in a shrill voice, to the
accompaniment of pulsating notes which intensify them by contrast?'

In all his canvases painted in the South Seas complementary colors,
orange and blue, yellow and violet, green and red, at their highest intensities and without modulation of values, are balanced harmoniously against
each other, forming beautiful, almost abstract patterns. *Fatata te Miti*,
which means 'by the sea,' is a masterpiece of the painter's newly created
style, in which he uses colors as arbitrarily as a composer uses sound. It
may have been this picture which Mallarmé, the symbolist poet, had in
mind when he said of a canvas by his friend Gauguin, 'It is a musical
poem, it needs no libretto.' Collections: Ambroise Vollard, Paris; Louis
Horch, New York. *Chester Dale Collection*, 1942. Signed, and dated 1892.

HENRI DE TOULOUSE-LAUTREC (French, 1864–1901)

QUADRILLE AT THE MOULIN ROUGE   Gouache on cardboard
Catalogue No. D-73   Height 31½" (80 cm.)
                                     Width 23¾" (64 cm.)

After the opening of an art exhibition, Toulouse-Lautrec sent a friend his impressions with this note: 'What a crush!... A hurly-burly of gloved hands carrying pince-nez framed in tortoise-shell or gold... Here are some observations I made among all those elbows.' He saw the world at elbow height. He was a dwarf.

But there is no self-pity in his observations. He enjoyed the hurly-burly of men and women. Day and night he drew and painted his *comédie humaine*. For an artist who lived only thirty-seven years, the corpus of his work is enormous. More than any other painter he has given us our imagery of Paris and Parisians at the turn of the century. They are all there: writers, painters, singers, dancers, sportsmen, prostitutes, poor and rich, the whole crush of human beings looming above a tiny draftsman.

He was perhaps the last great artist to be preoccupied with humanity. Though he represented members of his own class – for he was a descendant of the Counts of Toulouse – the specifically human quality he sought was more apparent elsewhere. He found it strongest at the theater, at the races, in cabarets, in brothels, among artists and their impresarios, or among the vicious and their victims, wherever genius had left the strong lines of character or degradation, the numb look of indifference.

He was fascinated by spontaneous wickedness. He destroyed himself with dissipation and drink. 'He was,' Yvette Guilbert, the singer, once said, 'the genius of deformity.' But he drew the strange contours, both physical and spiritual, of the men and women he portrayed with the same witty detachment he showed towards his own illness. He made no moral comment. He retained at all times his impersonal vision.

Painted in 1892, the figures in *Quadrille at the Moulin Rouge* have been identified, from left to right, as Valentin le Désossé, Mlle Lucie Bellanger, and Gabrielle, a dancer in Montmartre. The painting once belonged to Louis Bouglé, who posed for several portraits. He was a bicycle enthusiast and a member of the sporting set of Tristan Bernard. Collections: Louis Bouglé, Paris. *Chester Dale Collection*, 1942. Signed with monogram. Painted 1892.

HENRI ROUSSEAU (French, 1844–1910)
THE EQUATORIAL JUNGLE   Canvas
Catalogue No. D-70   Height 55¼" (140.3 cm.)
                                                Width 51" (129.5 cm.)

It is significant that an obscure inspector of customs should have changed the course of painting in our time almost as much as Michelangelo or Rubens did in theirs. None of the Post-Impressionists, with the possible exception of Cézanne, anticipated or influenced the direction of the modern French School to the same degree as did the self-taught Rousseau. His admirers and disciples included most of the leading artists of the first quarter of the twentieth century: Picasso, Braque, Derain, de Chirico, Vlaminck, to mention a few. For Rousseau brought to painting the qualities that these artists had lost: directness of vision, innocence of technique, and naïveté of spirit. He was one of the very few unself-conscious painters of modern times.

It is surprising to find that Rousseau considered his paintings realistic, but we know from many sources that he wished to render nature accurately and that he envied the academic painters their greater skill. But still more important than realism to his mind was the artist's emotional response to his vision. Apollinaire, the French poet, describes how the *douanier,* when painting a terrifying subject, would quite genuinely become frightened by his own creation and rush trembling to open a window. His pictures had for him a life of their own. He once said that he did not mind sleeping in his uncomfortable studio for, as he put it, 'You know, when I wake up I can smile at my canvases.'

And it is this curious inner life which makes *The Equatorial Jungle,* which he painted in 1909 the year before his death, so fascinating a picture. The wilderness Rousseau depicts is overfecund and sinister. Leaves and flowers are magnified even beyond the fantastic fertility of the tropics. Interwoven and interlocking, they form a barrier and convey a sense of the impenetrability of the jungle. Within this jungle and furtively peering out is a hidden life, menacing and full of small sounds. The rhythmic beauty of the repeated leaf shapes in Rousseau's landscape is extraordinary, and as a decorator he is difficult to surpass; but the real wonder of the painting lies in its imaginative realism, in its powerful conception, in the degree to which the artist is possessed by his subject until the scene he depicts comes alive in a strange, almost magical way. Collections: Robert Delaunay, Paris. *Chester Dale Collection,* 1942. Signed, and dated 1909.

244

LINTON PARK (American, 1826–1906)   Bed ticking
FLAX SCUTCHING BEE
Catalogue No. 1227   Height 31¼″ (79.5 cm.)   Width 50¼″ (127.7 cm.)

Rousseau would have felt sympathy and understanding for the American folk-painters. These self-taught and often anonymous artists who flourished chiefly in the nineteenth century, though talented practitioners are to be found from earliest Colonial times, established a native style.

There are many designations of this style, the most satisfactory of which seems to be primitive painting. It is a method of delineation that is realistic but not naturalistic. It is an objective statement of fact to which lack of technical accomplishment adds a touch of fantasy. It is an idea of a person, a place, or an object, around which the artist, so to speak, puts a line. But such representation is rarely achieved without a certain stress and strain. Part of the charm of these pictures lies in the tension between a recalcitrant image and the artist's determination to get it down on his canvas or panel.

Flax Scutching Bee represents a gathering of neighbors to prepare flax for weaving into linen — a task known as scutching.   *Continued on page 248*

GEORGE INNESS (American, 1825–1894)   Canvas
THE LACKAWANNA VALLEY
Catalogue No. 779   Height 33⅞″ (86 cm.)   Width 50⅛″ (127.3 cm.)

Recently on an ever-increasing scale the patronage of art has come from commercial firms; and the ancient problem of the relation between patron and artist, how much the one should dictate and the other acquiesce, has arisen again. In painting the roundhouse at Scranton for the Delaware and Lackawanna Railroad in 1855, George Inness was confronted with this immemorial conflict. He painted one picture and it was unsatisfactory. He had shown only one line of rails, all that existed at the time, but the president of the railroad wanted him to show the additional three or four planned for the future. Also he was told to depict four trains, the entire rolling stock of the company, and to paint the letters D. L. & W. on a locomotive. He protested as an artist but gave in as the head of a family. He needed the seventy-five dollars he was to be paid. Later the railroad sold the painting, and Inness as an old man recovered it in a junk shop in Mexico.

Who is right, railroad or artist? Most people today would stand behind
Continued on page 255

ALBERT PINKHAM RYDER (American, 1847–1917)
SIEGFRIED AND THE RHINE MAIDENS   Canvas
Catalogue No. 886   Height 19⁷/₈″ (50.5 cm.)
                                           Width 20¹/₂″ (52 cm.)

'Dim vales–and shadowy floods–
And cloudy-looking woods'

Where in art is there a more perfect embodiment of the landscapes of Edgar
Allan Poe's tortured imagination than the canvases of Albert Pinkham
Ryder? His works are the most poetic in American painting. A recluse
known to only a few artists and connoisseurs, most of his life was spent
in a dusty New York studio. There he painted his visionary scenes, working and reworking the pigment on his canvases until his thick, creamy
impasto became a glowing, prismatic substance. He wrote verse himself
and often his pictures have a literary theme. *Siegfried and the Rhine Maidens*
was begun immediately after the artist had returned from a performance of
Wagner's *Goetterdaemmerung*. Ryder told a friend, 'I worked for forty-
eight hours without sleep or food, and the picture was the result.' It shows
Siegfried in armor riding in the moonlight, while the Rhine maidens from
the river beg him for his magic ring.

The treatment of the theme is remarkably abstract with details of the
figures and landscapes eliminated or simplified into large masses only
vaguely related to actual appearance. Yet there is enough reality in this
eerie, spellbound world to entrap the imagination, like some dimly-re-
membered dream, which half-persuades the dreamer of its actuality. This
is the principal object of the Romantic style in art, of which *Siegfried and
the Rhine Maidens* is a superb example. Collections: Sir William Cornelius
Van Horne, Montreal. *Mellon Collection,* 1946. Painted between 1875 and
1891, when it was first exhibited in New York.

Continued from page 247
Linton Park, the artist of the picture, was at one time a builder and
these details of construction are rendered with particular accuracy. He was
also a furniture maker, an occupation needed to eke out his livelihood, for
as a painter he received only ten dollars for the picture reproduced. Collections: John Houk, Indiana, Pa.; Mrs Nanny Sedgwick, St Louis, Mo.; Houk
Hotel, Indiana, Pa.; *Gift of Edgar William and Bernice Chrysler Garbisch*
from their collection of American primitive paintings, 1953. Painted
c. 1850–55.

248

THOMAS EAKINS (American, 1844–1916)   Canvas
THE BIGLEN BROTHERS RACING   Height 24″ (61 cm.)
Catalogue No. 1180   Width 36″ (91.5 cm.)

Thomas Eakins was the most intellectual artist America has produced, and yet *The Biglen Brothers Racing* which he painted probably in 1873 looks at first glance as fortuitous and casual as a colored snapshot. Where did the intellectual element in Eakins' painting show itself? What is the difference between a realistic painting of this kind and a good color photograph? Though Eakins himself was a pioneer photographer, he used the camera only as a mechanical means of gathering data about appearance, not as a basis for his pictures. Actually this scene of a rowing race about to begin was put together in the studio from sketches and from memory. The picture seems photographic because painter and camera have the same goal, to show, as Eakins said, 'What o'clock it is, afternoon or morning, winter or summer, and what kind of people are there, and what they are doing and why they are doing it.'

Continued on page 256

WINSLOW HOMER (American, 1836–1910)   Canvas
BREEZING UP   Height 24⅛″ (61.5 cm.)
Catalogue No. 760   Width 38⅛″ (97 cm.)

The distinguished achievement of American painting in the second half of the nineteenth century was due in no small part to Winslow Homer, who shares with Thomas Eakins a pre-eminent position in the tradition of American realism. Homer was trained as an illustrator, and an element of illustration appears in his pictures from beginning to end. His earliest significant work was drawn for *Harper's Weekly* during the Civil War, when he was detailed to the Army of the Potomac as a correspondent. Working for a magazine, he learned to make his illustrations clear and specific. Throughout his life he presented his subjects graphically with a keen sense of actuality. Such objective recording has now almost vanished from art; and Homer's pictorial style with its simple, lucid statements has had little if any influence in recent years.

Yet Homer was able to suggest mood, feeling, atmosphere, as vividly as any Abstract Expressionist. Three small boys and a fisherman in a sailboat evoke the pleasure of sailing before a fair breeze; a dory with men peering over the side into a foggy sky conveys the loneliness and vastness of the

Continued on page 256

251

JAMES Mc WHISTLER (American, 1834–1903)

THE WHITE GIRL   Canvas

Catalogue No. 750   Height 84¹/₂″ (214.7 cm.)

Width 42¹/₂″ (108 cm.)

There have always been two opposed traditions in American painting. Eakins and Homer represent one: a rugged native vitality; Whistler and Mary Cassatt illustrate the second: a genteel, Europeanized urbanity. Though Whistler's fame is brighter in Europe than in America, his sophisticated selection of what seems best, wherever found, is of exceptional significance to this country, for it marks the coming of age of American painting.

Whistler would never have understood or approved of Homer's or Eakins' works. He tried to avoid what they sought, qualities he described as 'damned realism, and beautiful nature and the whole mess.' He preached a return to 'that wondrous thing called the masterpiece, which surpasses in perfection all that they (the gods) have contrived in what is called Nature.' In other words, Whistler wished to demonstrate that the inventive force of the artist is more important than the recording power of his eye. To do this he combined the patterns of Japanese prints with that mastery of value relations which distinguishes the painting of Velázquez. This eclecticism is predictable from even so early a work as *The White Girl*, a portrait of his mistress Joanna Heffernan. It was shown in 1863 at the Salon des Refusés with what we now consider to be many of the finest French paintings of the second half of the nineteenth century. It proved to be the sensation of that exhibition, the most revolutionary held in France in a hundred years.

True, the public was hostile, and Zola has reported how people nudged one another and became almost hysterical with indignation in front of the painting. But the wisest connoisseurs and critics were enthusiastic, and with *The White Girl* Whistler became the first American painter since the eighteenth century to attain renown and leadership among European artists. Collections: Thomas Whistler, Baltimore. *Harris Whittemore Collection*, 1943. Signed, and dated 1862.

MARY CASSATT (American, 1844–1926)
THE BOATING PARTY   Canvas
Catalogue No. D-38   Height 35½″ (90.2 cm.)
                                            Width 46¼″ (117.5 cm.)

How great a sacrifice should a woman make to become an artist? The life of Mary Cassatt poses this question. The daughter of wealthy parents, she renounced a conventional existence in America for a lifetime of study in Europe and a career of painting. In Paris she was early fascinated by the work of Degas, which she first saw in the window of a picture dealer. 'I used to go,' she wrote a friend, 'and flatten my nose against that window and absorb all I could of his art. It changed my life.' It spurred her to tireless self-discipline, especially in drawing. On seeing some of her work, Degas once said that he would not have admitted that a woman could draw so well. As for the use she made of her perfected technique, no one since the Renaissance has painted the relation of mother and child with such tender inventiveness. In pictures like the one reproduced, Miss Cassatt has brought a new interpretation to a traditional theme. She avoids the sentimental; she sees the mother as busy, proud of her child, but very matter-of-fact. This, and many similar canvases, will assure Miss Cassatt a high place in the history of painting. And yet after those long hours of physical labor at the easel, after the strain and the fight for recognition for her own work and the work of her friends, the Impressionists, was the sacrifice she made worthwhile? She ended her life a lonely woman, living in self-imposed exile, surrounded in her château by beautiful works of art which blindness, the lot of so many painters, prevented her from seeing. Miss Cassatt has left us the suggestion of an answer to the question of why maternity is the subject which occurs most frequently in her work. 'After all,' she said to a friend, 'woman's vocation in life is to bear children.' Collections: In the possession of the artist until at least 1914; Durand-Ruel, New York. *Chester Dale Collection*, 1942. Painted 1893–94 at Antibes.

Continued from page 247
the painter and say he should not be interfered with by his patrons. Yet many of the greatest works of art were executed in accordance with the strictest contracts, how many figures to be shown, where they were to stand, how much gold, how much blue, how much red to be used. Within this rigid framework the painter exerted his genius to create a work of beauty, and he succeeded more often in reaching his goal than many modern artists
Continued on page 256

Continued from page 251

But these facts the painter can convey more convincingly than the camera. A photograph taken on a sunny day indicates sunshine; but Eakins' careful study of reflected light taught him how to exaggerate the sparkle of sunlight on water until the waves seemed to catch the rays of the sun itself. A photograph indicates depth; but Eakins' precise perspective worked out mathematically, draws the spectator's vision into this depth, makes him part of the scene. And a photograph sometimes fixes in the kaleidoscope of appearance a satisfactory design; but it almost never achieves, as in *The Biglen Brothers Racing*, an integrated composition in which no object can be altered or removed without destroying the whole effect. Collections: Mrs Thomas Eakins; Whitney Museum of American Art, New York. *Gift of Mr and Mrs Cornelius Vanderbilt Whitney*, 1953. Painted probably

Continued from page 251

sea; a huntsman with his dog silhouetted against the mountain suggest the exhilaration of sport. One could elaborate endlessly.

But the important point is that a certain mood is induced in the spectator's mind by recognizable images. Representation in the visual arts is, of course, traditional. The basic language of painting with rare exceptions has always been representational, an imagery of identifiable objects. At times, however, painting has tried to usurp the function of other arts: poetry, for example, with the Pre-Raphaelites, and music with the Abstract Expressionists. With Winslow Homer, there is no confusion of the arts. He simply represents actual scenes with such vividness, with such grasp of significance, that their pervading mood is inescapable. Collections: Charles Stewart Smith, New York; Howard Caswell Smith, Oyster Bay, New York. *Gift of the W. L. and May T. Mellon Foundation*, 1943.

Continued from page 255

with a blank canvas and nothing to do but express their own ideas.

Commercial patronage may also have helped Inness. Out of the actual scene he was compelled to paint he has created a vision of ordered beauty. Today *The Lackawanna Valley* is more highly prized than the misty landscapes he painted at the end of his life, when he had no patron to dictate, no one to tell him that his statement, 'A work of art is beautiful if the sentiment is beautiful, it is great if the sentiment is vital,' is an over-simplification of the problem of painting. Collections: Delaware, Lackawanna & Western Railroad; Mrs Jonathan Scott Hartley, the artist's daughter, New York. *Gift of Mrs Huttleston Rogers*, 1945. Signed. Painted 1855.

Byzantine School, XIII Century   *Master of the Franciscan Crucifix*   *Cimabue* Christ
Madonna and Child Enthroned   St. John the Evangelist   Between St. Peter and St. James Major

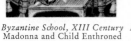

Margaritone   *Duccio di Buoninsegna*   *Follower of Giotto*
Madonna and Child Enthroned   Nativity with the Prophets Isaiah and Ezekiel   St. Paul

Bernardo Daddi Madonna   *Master of the Life of St. John the Baptist*   *Paolo Veneziano*
and Child with Saints and Angels   The Baptism of Christ   The Coronation of the Virgin

257

Simone Martini
St. John the Baptist

Lippo Memmi
Madonna and Child with Donor

Gentile da Fabriano
Madonna and Child

Fra Angelico The Healing of Palladia by
St. Cosmas and St. Damian

Domenico Veneziano
St. Francis Receiving the Stigmata

Gentile da Fabriano A Miracle
of St. Nicholas

Masolino da Panicale
The Annunciation

Domenico Veneziano
Madonna and Child

Giovanni di Paolo The Annunciation

Fra Filippo Lippi St. Benedict Orders St. Maurus
to the Rescue of St. Placidus

Fra Filippo Lippi
Madonna and Child

Piero della Francesca St. Apollonia

Andrea del Castagno Portrait of a Man

Benozzo Gozzoli The Dance of Salome

Francesco di Giorgio
God the Father Surrounded by Angels and Cherubins

Benvenuto di Giovanni
The Adoration of the Magi

Domenico Ghirlandaio
Madonna and Child

Sandro Botticelli Portrait of a Youth

Neroccio de' Landi and Master
of the Griselda Legend Claudia Quinta

Luca Signorelli
Eunostos of Tanagra

Circle of Verrocchio (possibly Leonardo)
Madonna and Child with a Pomegranate

Filippino Lippi Tobias and the Angel

Filippino Lippi Portrait of a Youth

Lorenzo di Credi Self-Portrait

Cosimo Tura Madonna
and Child in a Garden

Marco Zoppo Madonna and Child

Pisanello Profile Portrait of a Lady

Francesco del Cossa St. Florian

Francesco del Cossa St. Lucy

Francesco del Cossa The Crucifixion

Ercole Roberti
Giovanni II Bentivoglio

Giovanni Antonio Boltraffio
Portrait of a Youth

Ambrogio de'Predis
Bianca Maria Sforza

261

Antonello da Messina
Madonna and Child

Carlo Crivelli Madonna
and Child Enthroned with Donor

Antonello da Messina
Portrait of a Young Man

Carlo Crivelli Madonna and Child

Giovanni Bellini Orpheus

Giovanni Bellini The Flight into Egypt

Giovanni Bellini
Portrait of a Young Man in Red

262

Giovanni Bellini
Madonna and Child

Cima da Conegliano St. Jerome
in the Wilderness

Venetian Master
Portrait of a Young Man

Vittore Carpaccio Madonna and Child

Lorenzo Lotto A Maiden's Dream

Lorenzo Lotto The Nativity

Bernardino Luini
Procris' Prayer to Diana

Bernardino Luini Portrait of a Lady

263

Master of Flémalle and Assistants Madonna
and Child with Saints in the Enclosed Garden

Petrus Christus A Donor and His Wife

Master of St. Veronica
The Crucifixion

Hans Memling St. Veronica

Hans Memling
Portrait of a Man with an Arrow

Hans Memling
Chalice of St. John the Evangelist

Jan Gossaert (Mabuse)
St. Jerome Penitent

Miguel Sithium A Knight of the
Order of Calatrava

Joos van Cleve
Joris W. Vezeler

Joos van Cleve
Margaretha Boghe,
Wife of Joris W. Vezeler

Master of St. Gilles The Conversion
of an Arian by St. Rémy

Juan de Flandres The Annunciation

Bernhard Strigel Margaret Vöhlin,
Wife of Hans Rott

Bernhard Strigel Hans Rott,
Patrician of Memmingen

Albrecht Dürer Lot and His Daughters

Lucas Cranach the Elder
Portrait of a Man

Lucas Cranach the Elder
Portrait of a Woman

Lucas Cranach the Elder
A Princess of Saxony

Albrecht Altdorfer The Fall of Man

Antonis Mor
Portrait of a Gentleman

Lucas van Leyden The Card Players

Jan van Scorel The Rest on the Flight into Egypt

ITALIAN SCHOOL: XVI AND XVII CENTURY

Raphael Bindo Altoviti

Raphael
The Niccolini-Cowper Madonna

Andrea del Sarto Charity

Pontormo The Holy Family

Il Rosso Portrait of a Man

Correggio The Mystic Marriage of St. Catherine

Giorgione The Holy Family

Agnolo Bronzino A Young Woman and Her Little Boy

Giorgione and Titian Portrait of a Venetian Gentleman

Titian Vincenzo Capello

Titian Ranuccio Farnese

Titian St. John the Evangelist on Patmos

Sebastiano del Piombo
Portrait of a Young Woman as a Wise Virgin

Sebastiano del Piombo
Portrait of a Humanist

Paris Bordone The Baptism
of Christ

Giovanni Girolamo Savoldo
Portrait of a Knight

Giovanni Battista Moroni
Gian Federico Madruzzo

Giovanni Battista Moroni
"Titian's Schoolmaster"

Jacopo Tintoretto Doge Alvise Mocenigo and Family
before the Madonna and Child

Paolo Veronese
The Finding of Moses

Paolo Veronese
The Annunciation

268

Paolo Veronse Rebecca at the Well

Michelangelo Caravaggio Still Life

Jan Lys The Satyr and the Peasant

Orazio Gentileschi St. Cecilia and an Angel

SPANISH SCHOOL: XVI AND XVII CENTURY

El Greco St. Ildefonso

El Greco St. Jerome

El Greco St. Martin and the Beggar

Zurbarán St. Jerome with St. Paula and St. Eustochium

Bartolomé Esteban Murillo
The Return of the Prodigal Son

Juan de Valdés Leal
The Assumption of the Virgin

269

Peter Paul Rubens Decius Mus Addressing
the Legions

Peter Paul Rubens
Marchesa Brigida Spinola Doria

Sir Anthony van Dyck
Marchesa Balbi

Sir Anthony van Dyck
Susanna Fourment and Her Daughter

Sir Anthony van Dyck
Portrait of a Flemish Lady

Sir Anthony van Dyck Filippo Cattaneo,
Son of Marchesa Elena Grimaldi

Sir Anthony van Dyck Clelia Cattaneo,
Daughter of Marchesa Elena Grimaldi

Sir Anthony van Dyck
Giovanni Vincenzo Imperiale

Sir Anthony van Dyck
The Prefect, Raphael Racius

Sir Anthony van Dyck Paola Adorno,
Marchesa Brignole Sale and Her Son

Sir Anthony van Dyck
The Assumption of the Virgin

Sir Anthony van Dyck
Philip, Lord Wharton

Sir Anthony van Dyck
Henri II de Lorraine, Duc de Guise

Frans Hals
Portrait of an Elderly Lady

Frans Hals Portrait of an Officer

Frans Hals Portrait of a Young Man

Frans Hals Portrait of a Man

271

Frans Hals Portrait of a Gentleman

Frans Hals Portrait of a Man

Pieter Jansz. Saenredam
Cathedral of St. John
at 's-Hertogenbosch

Rembrandt van Ryn A Turk

Rembrandt van Ryn
Saskia van Uilenburgh, the Wife of the Artist

Rembrandt van Ryn
A Polish Nobleman

Rembrandt van Ryn
Study of an Old Man

Rembrandt van Ryn Self-Portrait

Rembrandt van Ryn
An Old Lady with a Book

Rembrandt van Ryn
The Philosopher

Rembrandt van Ryn
A Girl with a Broom

Rembrandt van Ryn
The Descent from the Cross

Rembrandt van Ryn
The Apostle Paul

Rembrandt van Ryn
A Woman Holding a Pink

Rembrandt van Ryn
Head of an Aged Woman

Rembrandt van Ryn Philemon and Baucis

Rembrandt van Ryn The Circumcision

273

Rembrandt van Ryn
Head of St. Matthew

Rembrandt van Ryn
A Young Man Seated at a Table

Rembrandt van Ryn
Portrait of a Man in a Tall Hat

Rembrandt van Ryn Portrait of
a Gentleman with a Tall Hat and Gloves

Rembrandt van Ryn Lucretia

Rembrandt van Ryn Portrait of
a Lady with an Ostrich-Feather Fan

Nicolas Maes
An Old Woman Dozing over a Book

Aelbert Cuyp
Herdsmen Tending Cattle

274

Jan Steen The Dancing Couple

Pieter de Hooch The Bedroom

Jan Vermeer The Girl with a Red Hat

Willem Kalf Still Life

Gabriel Metsu The Intruder

FRENCH AND ITALIAN SCHOOLS: XVII AND XVIII CENTURY

Simon Vouet The Muses Urania and Calliope

Nicolas Poussin The Baptism of Christ

275

Louis Le Nain
A French Interior

Philippe de Champagne
Omer Talon

Antoine Watteau
Ceres (Summer)

Nicolas Lancret La Camargo Dancing

Jean-Baptiste-Joseph Pater On the Terrace

Jean-Marc Nattier
Joseph Bonnier de la Mosson

Hubert Drouais Portrait of a Lady

Jean-Baptiste-Siméon Chardin
The House of Cards

276

Maurice-Quentin de la Tour
Claude Dupouch

Jean-Baptiste-Siméon Chardin
Soap Bubbles

Jean-Baptiste-Siméon Chardin
The Kitchen Maid

Charles-Amédée-Philippe van Loo
The Magic Lantern

François Boucher
Madame Bergeret

François Boucher The Love Letter

Elisabeth Vigée-Lebrun
Portrait of a Lady

Jean-Baptiste Greuze
Monsieur de La Live de Jully

François-Hubert Drouais
Group Portrait

277

Jean-Honoré Fragonard
The Swing

Hubert Robert The Old Bridge

Giovanni Battista Tiepolo
Scene from Roman History

Giovanni Battista Tiepolo Apollo Pursuing Daphne

Canaletto The Square of St. Mark's

Canaletto The Portello and the Brenta Canal at Padua

Bernardo Bellotto View of Munich

Pietro Longhi The Simulated Faint

Francesco Guardi View of the Rialto

Francesco Guardi
Campo San Zanipolo

278

George Stubbs
Colonel Pocklington with Sisters

Thomas Gainsborough
Master John Heathcote

Thomas Gainsborough
The Hon. Mrs. Graham

Thomas Gainsborough
Georgiana, Duchess of Devonshire

Sir Joshua Reynolds
Lady Betty Hamilton

Thomas Gainsborough
Landscape with a Bridge

Sir Joshua Reynolds
Squire Musters

Sir Joshua Reynolds
Lady Elizabeth Compton

Sir Joshua Reynolds Lady
Elizabeth Delmé and Her Children

George Romney
Lady Arabella Ward

John Hoppner
The Hoppner Children

Sir Henry Raeburn
Colonel Francis James Scott

Sir Thomas Lawrence
Lady Templetown and Her Son

John Crome ("Old Crome")
Harling Gate, near Norwich

George Morland
The End of the Hunt

John Singleton Copley
Epes Sargent

John Singleton Copley
The Red Cross Knight

Benjamin West The Battle of La Hogue

280

Ralph Earl
Daniel Boardman

Gilbert Stuart George Washington
(Vaughan Portrait)

Gilbert Stuart
Lady Liston

John Trumbull
Alexander Hamilton

SPANISH AND BRITISH SCHOOLS: XIX CENTURY

Goya Don Bartolomé Sureda

Goya Victor Guye

Goya Señora Sabasa Garcia

Goya (attributed to) Bullfight

John Constable The White Horse

John Constable A View of Salisbury Cathedral

J. M. W. Turner
The Junction of the Thames and the Medway

J. M. W. Turner
Keelmen Heaving in Coals by Moonlight

J. M. W. Turner
The Dogana and Santa Maria della Salute, Venice

FRENCH SCHOOL: XIX CENTURY

Jacques-Louis David
Madame David

Jean-Auguste-Dominique Ingres
Monsieur Marcotte

Jean-Auguste-Dominique Ingres
Pope Pius VII in the Sistine Chapel

Eugène Delacroix
Columbus and His Son at La Rábida

Jean-Baptiste-Camille Corot
Forest of Fontainbleau

Jean-Baptiste-Camille Corot
Ville d'Avray

Jean-Baptiste-Camille Corot
The Artist's Studio

Jean-Baptiste-Camille Corot Italian Girl

Honoré Daumier Hippolyte Lavoignat

Edouard Manet The Dead Toreador

Gustave Courbet La Grotte de la Loue

Eugène Boudin Return of the Terre-Neuvier

283

Edouard Manet Oysters

Edouard Manet
Madame Michel-Lévy

Berthe Morisot In the Dining Room

Auguste Renoir Mademoiselle Sicot

Auguste Renoir Diana

Auguste Renoir The Dancer

Auguste Renoir Woman with a Cat

Auguste Renoir Madame Henriot

Auguste Renoir
Bather Arranging Her Hair

Auguste Renoir Odalisque

Auguste Renoir Oarsmen at Chatou

Camille Pissarro Peasant Woman

Camille Pissarro
Boulevard des Italiens, Morning, Sunlight

Edgar Degas
Duke and Duchess of Morbilli

Edgar Degas The Races

Edgar Degas
Achille de Gas in the Uniform of a Cadet

Edgar Degas Before the Ballet

Edgar Degas Madame Camus   *Claude Monet* Banks of the Seine, Vétheuil

Claude Monet
Madame Monet under the Willows

Claude Monet
Vase of Chrysanthemums

Claude Monet
Rouen Cathedral, West Façade,
Sunlight

Henri Fantin-Latour
Portrait of Sonia

Paul Cézanne Vase of Flowers

Paul Cézanne Landscape in Provence

286

Paul Cézanne
The Artist's Son Paul

Paul Cézanne Louis Guillaume

Vincent van Gogh The Olive Orchard

Paul Gauguin
Self-Portrait

Henri de Toulouse-Lautrec
Alfred la Guigne

Henri de Toulouse-Lautrec
Maxime Dethomas

Odilon Redon
Evocation of Roussel

AMERICAN SCHOOL: XIX AND EARLY XX CENTURY

Thomas Sully
Lady with a Harp: Eliza Ridgely

Chester Harding Amos Lawrence

Thomas Eakins
Monsignor Diomede Falconio

287

Winslow Homer Hound and Hunter

Winslow Homer Right and Left

Mary Cassatt The Loge

Mary Cassatt
The Morning Toilet

James A. McNeill Whistler
L'Andalouse

William Merritt Chase A Friendly Call

John Singer Sargent Repose

George Bellows Both Members of This Club

Robert Henri
Young Woman in White

288

LIST OF ILLUSTRATIONS

Color plates are indicated by the page numbers in italic

289

293

DROUAIS, HUBERT (French, 1699–1767): *Portrait of a Lady.*
Canvas, 46¹/₂×37¹/₂″ (118×95 cm.). Catalogue No. 742.
Chester Dale Collection. 276

DUCCIO DI BUONINSEGNA (Sienese, active 1278–1319): *The Calling of the
Apostles Peter and Andrew.* Wood, 17¹/₈×18¹/₈″ (43.5×46 cm.).
Catalogue No. 252. Samuel H. Kress Collection. 67
Nativity with the Prophets Isaiah and Ezekiel. Wood.
Center panel, 17¹/₄×17¹/₂″ (43.8×44.4 cm.); each side panel, 17¹/₄×6¹/₂″
(43.8×16.5 cm.). Catalogue No. 8. Mellon Collection. 257

DÜRER, ALBRECHT (German, 1471–1528): Obverse: *Madonna and Child.* 112
Reverse: *Lot and His Daughters.* Wood, 19³/₄×15⁵/₈″ (50.2×39.7 cm.).
Catalogue No. 1099. Samuel H. Kress Collection. 265
Portrait of a Clergyman. Parchment on canvas, 16⁷/₈×13″ (42.9×33.2 cm.).
Catalogue No. 1100. Samuel H. Kress Collection. 114

DYCK, SIR ANTHONY VAN (Flemish, 1599–1641): *Portrait of a Flemish Lady.*
Canvas, 48³/₈×35¹/₂″ (123×90 cm.). Catalogue No. 500.
Mellon Collection. 270
Susanna Fourment and Her Daughter. Canvas, 68×46¹/₄″ (173×117 cm.).
Catalogue No. 48. Mellon Collection. 270
Marchesa Balbi. Canvas, 72×48″ (183×122 cm.). Catalogue No. 49.
Mellon Collection. 270
Marchesa Elena Grimaldi, Wife of Marchese Nicola Cattaneo.
Canvas, 97×68″ (246×173 cm.). Catalogue No. 688. Widener Collection. 158
Filippo Cattaneo, Son of Marchesa Elena Grimaldi.
Canvas, 48¹/₈×33¹/₈″ (122.2×84.2 cm.). Catalogue No. 689.
Widener Collection. 270
Clelia Cattaneo, Daughter of Marchesa Elena Grimaldi.
Canvas, 48¹/₈×33¹/₈″ (122×84 cm.). Catalogue No. 690.
Widener Collection. 270
Giovanni Vincenzo Imperiale. Canvas, 50×41¹/₂″ (127×105.5 cm.).
Catalogue No. 685. Widener Collection. 270
The Prefect, Raphael Racius. Canvas, 51⁵/₈×41⁵/₈″ (131×105.5 cm.).
Catalogue No. 686. Widener Collection. 271
Paola Adorno, Marchesa Brignole Sale and Her Son.
Canvas, 74¹/₂×55″ (189.5×139.5 cm.). Catalogue No. 687.
Widener Collection. 271
The Assumption of the Virgin. Canvas, 46¹/₂×40¹/₄″ (118×102 cm.).
Catalogue No. 684. Widener Collection. 271
Philip, Lord Wharton. Canvas, 52¹/₂×41⁷/₈″ (133×106 cm.).
Catalogue No. 50. Mellon Collection. 271
Henri II de Lorraine, Duc de Guise.
Canvas, 80⁵/₈×48⁵/₈″ (204.8×123.5 cm.). Catalogue No. 908.
Gift of Cornelius Vanderbilt Whitney. 271

EAKINS, THOMAS (American, 1844–1916): *The Biglen Brothers Racing.*
Canvas, 24×36″ (61.2×91.6 cm.). Catalogue No. 1180.
Gift of Mr. and Mrs. Cornelius Vanderbilt Whitney. 250
Monsignor Diomede Falconio. Canvas, 72¹/₈×54¹/₄″ (183.2×37.8 cm.).
Catalogue No. 889. Gift of Stephen C. Clark. 287

EARL, RALPH (American, 1751–1801): *Daniel Boardman.*
81⁵/₈×55⁵/₁₆″ (207.5×140.5 cm.). Catalogue No. 1026.
Gift of Mrs. W. Murray Crane. 281

EYCK, JAN VAN (Flemish, 1380/1400–1441): *The Annunciation.* Transferred
from wood to canvas, 36¹/₂×14³/₈″ (93×36.5 cm.). Catalogue No. 39.
Mellon Collection. 92